To my family, Simon, Sonny, Buddy, Rocky, Lulu.

Thank you for your support, love and general awesomeness x

Janey Lee Grace's lively and deftly recounted behind-the-scenes memoir is funny, fascinating yet sobering too – loved it!
Freya North, *Sunday Times* best-selling author

I absolutely loved this book. Right from page 1, I just couldn't put it down. Each page just begged me to turn over to see what happens next. A funny, entertaining, and captivating read.
Dr David R Hamilton, author of *Why Woo-Woo Works*

Brimming with warmth, humour, gossip and glamour, this book is a peep behind the scenes of showbiz but also the story of a strong woman who grabs life with both hands and makes the most of every opportunity, whilst never being afraid to show her vulnerability. It's as honest and unflinching as it is inspirational – and hugely entertaining.
Veronica Henry, author of bestselling lifestyle fiction

Janey's book is a time capsule you have to open.
Anthea Turner, TV Presenter

Janey Lee Grace has had more careers than most people I know but as she says herself in her new book From Wham! to Woo: A Life on the Mic. *She has always been at the forefront of popular culture, lifestyle trends and her extraordinary journey to sobriety and wellbeing, as well as behind the mic. Janey's journey is an inspiration and reflection for so many of us and her story is certainly not nearly over yet!*
Lynne Franks, Writer and Founder of SEED Women's Empowerment Network

If you've ever imagined singing on Top of the Pops, *touring with Wham! or being on the radio with Steve Wright, you need to read Janey Lee Grace's memoir.*
Clare Pooley, *New York Times* best-selling author

This memoir is a fantastic 80's and 90's blast through the lens of Janey's fascinating career. A fun insight into the back rooms of pop music, TV and Radio.
Jo Wood, author, TV personality and former model

FROM WHAM! TO WOO ...

A Life on the Mic

JANEY LEE GRACE

McNIDDER & GRACE

Published by McNidder & Grace
21 Bridge Street
Carmarthen SA31 3JS
Wales, United Kingdom

www.mcnidderandgrace.com

Original paperback first published 2024

Image credits: page 12 of plate section, Mike Putland. Page 62, Gregg Eisman (both pics). Page 74, Joe Bangay. All other images supplied from the author's archive.

Some names and identifying details have been changed to protect the privacy of the people involved.

A catalogue record for this work is available from the British Library.

ISBN: 9780857162748
Ebook: 9780857162755

Cover: Tabitha Palmer
Designer: JS Typesetting Ltd
Printed and bound in the United Kingdom by Short Run Press, Exeter

CONTENTS

Chapter 1
A RAY OF SUNSHINE

It was baking hot on the roof of the Sebel Townhouse in Sydney. I wasn't sure how long I could fry my skin without burning, but I was acutely aware of just how glorious it felt to be lounging on a sunbed, waiters hovering nearby to ply me with drinks, and nothing to do till our soundcheck later that evening. Lying next to me (not *with* me) in tiny swimming trunks, very big and expensive sunglasses, earphones, and nothing else, was Rod Stewart who seemed to share none of my concerns about his skin getting burnt, wrinkled and haggard. He already had a deep tan, while I, having come from a wet cold winter in the UK, was lily-white and already starting to go the colour of beetroot in unsightly patches.

Later that day, after a quick shopping trip in the Kings Cross area of Sydney, I thought I'd check out the hotel spa. It was pretty empty; in fact, the only other person in the hot tub was my 'boss', George Michael. I hesitated for a second in case he wanted privacy, but he gave me one of his heart-stopping beaming smiles and said, 'Janey, come in!'

We sat there luxuriating in the bubbles and he asked how I was finding my first trip to Australia (his too). I told him I LOVED it. I felt so at home in Sydney, I'd even consider living here. He looked directly at me. George had a way of looking at you so that you knew he was going to mean what he said: 'Why don't you stay? You'd do great out here, I can really see you as a Bondi Beach girl. There's probably loads of work for singers, and if you're open to it, there is one of our Aussie film crew who'd be keen to showing you around.' He sort of winked as he said it. I was a bit shocked. Little insecure me thought he may have been suggesting I leave the tour or give up on my dreams of being a pop star to marry someone in the crew and be a kept woman. I had a pathological hatred of the idea of being a 'woman who lunched'. I was fiercely independent, and I wondered if he was suggesting I didn't have enough talent for anything more. Many years later, we laughed about that conversation. He said he had been waiting for an opportunity to tentatively suggest that I might want to live out there, as one of the cameramen definitely had the hots for me and George had promised he'd sound it out!

I wasn't romantically interested in that guy, but I can't deny I left a piece of my heart behind in Sydney. Had it been the last leg of Wham!'s tour rather than midway before heading to the US, I may well have said: 'Sod it all' and found a way to stay on. I fell in love with Sydney quickly because within a few hours of landing, I got chatting to an air steward. I could kick myself that I can't remember his name, but he was so nice and a big Wham! fan, and he offered to show me around. I seem to remember making it super clear I was spoken for, but he was cool, and as soon as we'd checked into the hotel, he zoomed me round Bondi Beach on a motorbike, then to a barbie where I met some of his friends, who were just lovely. I also told him I wanted to go to church. I think that surprised him a bit, but he connected me with a lovely woman who drove me from the hotel that Sunday morning to a church that was way too happy-clappy for me, but nevertheless, I got my fix of remembering I had a faith.

I thought about that conversation with George a fair bit during that tour in 1985 and as we flew back home six weeks later, I couldn't help but wonder if I shouldn't have just finished the final US leg and gone straight back to Australia. I recall lounging in my business class seat being wined and dined, and realising that within 24 hours, I'd be dragging my sorry arse and a big suitcase onto the Piccadilly line to travel back to my shared rental flat where nothing awaited me, other than half a can of baked beans in the fridge growing a fur coat.

The contrasts were sharp. As a backing singer with Wham! I lived a life of luxury – and, in fairness, without much of the responsibility. As jobs for singers go, you couldn't really top it.

Chapter 2
STARS IN HER EYES

It was watching ABBA win Eurovision with 'Waterloo' that made me want to be a pop singer. I sat so close to the TV that my dad told me to 'shift back, or you'll get square eyes.' But I was transfixed by the costumes, the style, the glamour and the harmonies. I loved singing. I'd cottoned on at an early age that it came naturally to me, and I didn't have to try hard to remember tunes or lyrics. At Sunday school, they desperately wanted to encourage the children to sing in the service, but everyone was too shy. They started bribing us with a few pence and sweets if we sang a solo. I liked the sound of that, and popped up regularly – so often, in fact, that I got quite rich for a seven-year-old (probably the beginnings of my dental issues in later life). After a while, they changed their bribe to a gift of a reading book for every few solos. In fairness, that suited me better because I also loved reading. In the style of Matilda, I didn't exactly have parents who encouraged reading. I did, however, have a local library and got through my full allowance of titles every three weeks.

Reading was my ticket, my window into a world much bigger than our subpar little council house in Stapleford (a not exactly salubrious corner of Nottingham). The expectations for me were that I would stay in the local area, working in the haberdasher's shop or the pencil factory. But I think I knew from as early as I can remember that I was destined for something else. Ambition fizzed around me. I was definitely not a show-off – in reality, insecure and unsure of myself – but I knew deep down that I wouldn't be sticking around.

My parents weren't unkind, or cruel, but both had mental health issues which meant they simply weren't able to provide the love and security I needed. I'll share more about that later.

Most people can cite one person who made a big impact on their life, and for me, it was my junior schoolteacher, Mr David Swainston. T. Rex had just hit the charts and I thought I'd died and gone to heaven. Watching Marc

At Skegness Beach

Bolan on *Top of the Pops* was like a bolt of electricity running through me, and I became fixated on his music. Mr Swainston played guitar and sang, and when he found out how much I loved the band, he seemed quite surprised but learned to play 'Ride a White Swan' on his acoustic and accompanied me one day singing in the school assembly. Totally crap it was, I'm sure, but I didn't care, he was a lifeline for me. He used to help me find sheet music so that I could learn lyrics or play lines on the recorder (the sum total of my musicianship skills for many years). And just how cool is it that you can just Google and download music manuscripts now! In chatting to him, I think I started to realise that maybe, *just maybe*, I could do something other than lay out rolls of fabric or collect the pencil shavings. He made life seem exciting. Things started to feel possible.

When I attended the Sunday school for the aforementioned sweets and books, somehow along the way, some of the messages sunk in. I kept on going to church right up until I left home. I bought it, all of it, and while I wasn't quite sure if I could ever be a born-again Christian, I liked the security of thinking God had my back. Also, the church gave me a social life. While some of the girls in my secondary school seemed to like hanging about in dodgy alleyways and getting themselves pregnant (there was an inordinate number of unwanted pregnancies at my sink-level secondary school) I stuck to my church crowd – well, a duo to be precise. My friend Karen and I attended church religiously (excuse the pun – attending was the only bit we did religiously), hoping for an introduction to the teens' club that we'd heard so much about. The joyful moment came when I was 13. A lovely middle-aged couple, Gerald and Dorothy who had a son a few years older than us, took us along to

Mum (Norma) and Dad (Alan)

Derby Youth for Christ, and they held church services with live music and 'charismatic speakers'. Karen and I were so excited! I had saved enough money to buy make-up and a maxi dress from Laura Ashley. I remember it clearly, the first dress I ever bought, and I wore a flower in my hair. There were not delighted, but what could my parents say? We were being picked up and delivered back on a Saturday night by a respectful, churchgoing, God-fearing couple.

The church was packed, with teenagers making up at least 60 percent of the congregation. Karen and I had never imagined that we might meet boys in a church situation! This was like manna from heaven. We sang a few boring hymns, listened to a very trendy vicar share some stuff, and then the room darkened. Showbiz time. A full lightshow and a mirrorball kicked in over the stage, and on came the first live band.

Writz were a proper electro pop band, possibly a bit ahead of their time, with a bit of punk thrown in. One of the lead singers, Steve Fairnie looked like a young Charlie Chaplin (he later made a film on the theme) and they had a cool gaunt looking bass player called Jules. I don't remember seeing the drummer from my seat, but it sounded great. Onto the stage strutted Bev Sage (Steve's wife, I later discovered) and Buzzy (Jule's wife). Bev had a shock of dyed white blonde hair while Buzzy's was bright red, and they wore the funkiest outfits I'd ever seen, including striped leg warmers and high heels!

That was it, my very first experience of live pop music. I loved it, and I knew I wanted to perform myself. I wanted to be in that spotlight. My head had literally been turned, but how could I get started? How could I widen my horizons, especially when my own parents were not exactly the adventurous types! How could I do something different – maybe even leave home?

The answer, at least to the last question, came in the form of my first proper boyfriend, Mark, who I met at Derby Youth for Christ. He first spotted me across the pews, then in the coffee hall afterwards shovelling in custard creams. He knew Gerald and Dorothy's son Rob and asked Rob to put a word in for him (seems like a theme), but I hadn't even noticed him in the crowd, so I don't remember responding.

A few more Youth for Christ events later, Valentine's Day came, and I received a card through the post. An actual

Valentine's Card – and I didn't know who it was from, I really didn't! It said something cryptic about YFC, but there were hundreds of guys there. I told a few school friends, all insane with jealousy, but they said it was probably just from my brother (I didn't have one) or even my sister. She had her ticket to a different life by now, being eight years older than me and already married to her childhood sweetheart.

That evening a friend dragged me along to a Valentine's disco in the local village hall. I was dreading it: I didn't drink (now I think about it, thank God I didn't start that early) and I hated the look of the spotty lanky youths doing the Bump or whatever hideous dance trend was going down. I couldn't wait for it to end so that my friend's dad would collect us (my parents didn't drive). Unbeknown to me, the sender of the card, Mark, had wondered why I hadn't responded, and with a confidence way beyond his 19 years, drove over to my house and knocked on the door. Rumour has it that my mum welcomed him joyfully and told him that I was at the local disco, while my dad (after rushing to put his dentures in and his shirt on) silently fumed at him in a *Don't think about going near my daughter* kind of way. And then into the seedy, horrible, cheap cider-swilling, sticky-carpeted and smoke-ridden disco of spotty kids entered this stunning, self-assured guy with long dark hair, gorgeous eyes and a captivating smile. Everyone stared as he walked straight up to me, told me how he knew I was there, and asked why I hadn't contacted him after receiving the card. I shrugged and said I didn't know who'd sent it, but all I could think about was whether meeting my parents and seeing my less than perfect home had already put him off! As he drove me home in his little Mini Cooper (he had a car!), I knew life would never be the same.

Mark wrote and sung in a Christian band, gigging in churches at weekends while working full time as an apprentice for a big-time prestigious engineering company. He took me to meet his parents in Buckinghamshire and that was my first introduction to a 'proper' family, a lovely home, wholesome cooking and all. We became inseparable.

* * *

Secondary school was a truly horrible girls only in Stapleford called Arthur Mee, and I hated it with a vengeance. With a staggering number of girls leaving to have babies, the exam results were appalling even for those of us who tried their best. I was not especially bullied because I was good at art, so that gave me a badge of honour, especially if a mean girl wanted their portrait done. I was once in a domestic science class, hating every second because I couldn't cook or sew, and the teacher was getting hugely frustrated as I tried to thread a needle, when I was summoned to the headmistress's office. Fearing the worst, I knocked on her door. She ushered me in with a smile, and then presented me with a pad, paper and pencils, saying, 'Draw my portrait, and make sure there are no wrinkles or age spots.' Well, it got me out of a class I hated.

I was beyond excited after being accepted to a sixth-form college in Nottingham for A levels. I think it was because my art portfolio was good, so they gave me the benefit of the doubt. I met Alison while waiting at the bus stop on the first day, and we instantly had a conversation about ballet, tap dancing (we both attended classes), pop music (we both loved it) and going to church (yes, we tentatively shared that we both did that too!). Alison is my 'longest-serving' friend to this day.

Winning a national Art Competition –
prize was a weekend in London!

With my best friend Alison on our first flight

Because Alison's parents had a car and were very supportive, they drove us to our first gig a couple of months later. We saw the Police at Derby Academy. Oh man, I still remember it. How can three guys make a sound like that? We got the bug then, and next came Elvis Costello with John Cooper Clarke as support. 'Why do you want to see Abbot and Costello?' was my dad's very old-style joke. Somehow, we got to go backstage and meet the guys, no idea how.

Fast-forward a few years and despite being very good at art and being offered a place on an art foundation course in Oxford, I opted to do a BA Honours in Performance Arts. My parents wanted me to go to Nottingham Uni (of course they did), but I had bigger ideas. Mark drove me to London (who has a boyfriend who does that?) and then went off to be a tourist, while I investigated Middlesex Poly – or as it later became known, Middlesex University – on the Trent Park site near Cockfosters. I walked through the glorious array of daffodils outside the mansion house and knew instinctively I'd found my place.

My audition day was like an assault on the senses. I'd never seen so many colourful, weird and wacky people! We did all kinds of icebreakers, and for the first time in 17 years I realised how tiny my world had been. This was my first experience of other cultures. There was one Black family in our town – I kid you not – but this room was full of exotic accents and sultry looks. I did a modern dance class that rocked my world, took part in a group improvisation where I had to be a fag end (yep, it was drama school) and laughed and sang till my throat was hoarse. I had a one-to-one interview and decided that I'd opt for dance rather than music; I had only minimal skills as a classical guitarist and singer, and I had been doing ballet and contemporary dance for years. When Mark collected me at the end of the day, I was exhilarated. I'd arrived.

I remember thinking he looked a little pale when he realised I'd be there for three years; he was rather hoping that I'd follow him out to whichever far-flung corner of the globe his firm might send him. Er… no. Although we were inseparable, this might have been the first seeds that would grow into the realisation that life with Mark wasn't forever.

Ballet Class at Trent Park

Chapter 3
BUGGER ALL IN PRATTING ABOUT

I loved my time at university. In those days, it was completely free for someone in my position with parents who had very little, and I got a decent grant. I found I could easily live on that and even save a bit for a rainy day. We affectionately referred to our wonderful degree course – BA Honours in Performance Arts (BAPA) – as 'Bugger All in Pratting About'. A degree in showing off for sure, and if you'd arrived in our refectory at any break or lunch time, you'd have thought you were in an episode of *Fame*. It was not uncommon for the dance students to suddenly jump up from eating their lettuce leaves to do a quick pirouette or sashay across the hall if they had an idea for some choreography, or if they wanted to show their new-found knowledge of Alvin Ailey (a contemporary dance choreographer), and there was always a table breaking into song. The other non-performance arts university students (I seem to remember there was a large engineering contingent) thought that us BAPAs were nuts.

Kev Baker, a funny, quick-witted Northerner with a mad professor-like shock of red hair, was my dearest friend at uni. He was such a talented actor and director with a zest for life that I hadn't encountered in anyone else. We did cinema all-nighters (Woody Allen and the original *Star Wars* trilogy), fairgrounds, loads of gigs and everything tourists in London do, despite our uni digs being right at the end of the Piccadilly line. I spent lots of weekends with Alison too, as she had gone to study music at Manchester Uni, and if I came home for holidays, we spent all our time together.

I was still with Mark – allegedly. By then he had risen through the ranks and been offered a job with his company in the UAE. When he started talking about me coming out there, once my degree was finished, to 'maybe start a dance school with the ex-pats', I don't think I was able to hide my horror. I suppose that he thought I'd come round – who wouldn't want to live in relative luxury, no expenses? He had a big salary from the company, as well as all his accommodation and living covered, but it wasn't very rock 'n' roll,

Bugger all in Pratting About (Kev on the left – me at the top)

was it? We tried to sustain a long-distance relationship for a good while. In fact, one Christmas when he came back to the UK, we got engaged. The whole thing was a bit bizarre, and I felt like I was observing myself playing a role. It lasted about five minutes.

One day, he summoned me to meet his boss at the firm's headquarters, so I put my best 'normal' outfit on. Even the lift to the penthouse office suite at the company headquarters seemed bigger than my flat, and I couldn't help but be impressed. What I hadn't expected, as we shook hands with Mark's boss, was that he would usher only me into his office, giving Mark a wave as if they'd already planned the conversation. Mark's eyes spoke silently to me, saying: 'Make it happen... don't blow it for me.'

We made small talk. *How lovely that Mark was able to make it to the UK, albeit briefly… The weather was agreeable for this time of year...* I remember feeling a bit on edge: *Why had I been asked here?* I knew the importance of body language, and didn't want to appear nervous, so I adjusted my position in the chair to mirror his. 'Tell me more about… Janey," he said as if he wanted me to describe a character in a novel. 'Mark tells me you are involved in… popular music, and er… dance,' he added, making it sound as though I was a travelling minstrel or a music-hall singer. 'Lovely,' he smirked. I prided myself even then on sussing people out, my sense of intuition was strong, but I couldn't yet see why he needed to spend a precious 15 minutes of his time making small talk with me. 'Congratulations again on your engagement,' he said. 'Will you continue to do the music and dance as a hobby? Amateur societies, choirs, a little dance troupe, that sort of thing, when you're married to Mark?' My intuition was fast kicking in, but I kept calm. 'It's my profession,' I told him, watching his amiable face slowly morph into a colder, harder expression as he explained to me that the wives of senior consultants such as Mark have to be 100 per cent supportive of their husbands. I stopped short of saying, 'And of course the husband will be wholly supportive of their wives' careers too.'

Suddenly, I had a moment of absolute clarity; this really was like something out of *The Stepford Wives*. He had called me in to make me understand in no uncertain terms that if he was investing in Mark, he couldn't have that commitment sidetracked by a loose cannon, a wife with – God forbid – a career. Worse than that, ambition! He continued, explaining how all-consuming being the wife of a senior employee would be. I'd need to be excellent at managing affairs, entertaining colleagues, organising the prep schools, the sale of the house, finding the right home for us and our family. I swear he actually winked at the thought of us creating said family. It sounded like my idea of hell, and it quickly became clear that the life with Mark stretching out before me would be one of wanting for nothing materially but giving up everything, including who I really was. I was furious with Mark when I emerged from the meeting and gave him back the engagement ring. He took it without much of a fight. He'd made his choice.

Chapter 4
CHASING DREAMS

I spent my uni years immersing myself more and more in the world of theatre and music. For a while I thought I'd work in musical theatre, but the auditions were brutal. I got down to the last three girls in about four auditions in the West End before I realised I didn't even want to do eight shows a week for a prolonged time. I craved flexibility and variety.

I didn't want to pursue my dancing, either. I wasn't brilliant, to be honest. It's such hard work being a contemporary dancer. Most of my friends stayed thin by never eating and by smoking, and they spent their lives chasing dodgy dancing jobs abroad – which, ironically, was the quickest easiest way to get your Equity card back then. If you wanted to work in the arts or entertainment industry, you needed an Equity card – and to get an Equity card, you had to work. There were only a couple of routes to get the provisional card. One way was topless dancing in bars on cruise ships, etc., and the other was by performing in a show that 'came under' Equity conditions but didn't require an Equity card to work there. Tricky? I'll say!

I bought *The Stage* newspaper every week and scoured the ads; most were dodgy as hell. I responded to one ad for actresses for a new film. The details were very sketchy, but it did say it could lead to an Equity card, so off I trotted to the director's house in Surbiton. I shudder when I think back now: it was a seedy flat, and he looked grubby to say the least. After looking at my portfolio of photos, he said he would need to take a few test shots, so got out his camera and asked me to pose, 'Look this way…look that way… OK, now take off your top…' I made my excuses and left.

I spent a fair bit of time at the Christian Arts Centre Group, which was housed in a building near the Old Vic in Waterloo. I took part in some great acting workshops there and made some good friends. One guy I met was Peter Williams, who, even then, was clearly incredibly creative. He later became the lighting designer for U2. His flatmate, another Pete (we called him Pete Project for some reason I can't recall), was friends with Gary Numan. We visited Gary's house in Surrey one day, which was full of impressive furnishings and weird artefacts that he'd collected on his world tours. There in the hallway stood the famous piano he'd written 'Cars' on, and he proudly showed us how he'd moved around the keys and come up with the riff. He also proudly showed us his private plane, a light aircraft parked up in his garden. I don't know if his licence stretched to night flying, but I was certainly not going to risk a trip up in it, techno pop giant or not!

It's been well documented that Gary has Asperger's, and it was brave of him to share that. Back then, all I noticed about him was his attention to detail and the way he constantly checked everything. He had a landline phone permanently connected to his mum, who obviously lived close by, and he regularly checked stuff with her. It was sweet, really. Annoying, isn't it, that all this was long before smartphones; otherwise I'd have proof of having been a Numanoid for a few hours.

Through Pete Project, I was also introduced to a tall glam rocker with a big grin, called Haze. John Mabley was his real name, and he later became well known as Doktor Haze, ringmaster and director of the Circus of Horrors. Haze and I got along great – lots of people thought we were an item, but it wasn't quite like that. I often stayed at the flat with the Pete's but I slept on Haze's futon, while he slept in a coffin with a satin purple lining, I kid you not.

Haze was the epitome of a modern-day Greatest Showman. Back in the day, he modelled himself on his absolute hero (and mine) Marc Bolan, and he proudly showed me that he could fit into Marc's skinny silver jeans that he'd bought at a vintage fair. His band was called Flash Harry, and they'd do gigs at the Empire, the Marquee and various other small clubs. They didn't really need backing vocals, but every now and then he'd find a role for me and I'd ladle on the make-up, borrow one of Haze's feather boas and have a fabulous glam time. We made an interesting pair around town, Haze with his long wavy hair, full make-up and long satin coats, plus lace-up boots, and me with leather miniskirts, corset-style tops and Dr Martens.

Haze co-founded the Circus of Horrors with Gerry Cottle in 1995. It debuted at Glastonbury and became Britain's longest-running alternative circus. In 2011, he released his autobiography book *Dr Haze: Mud, Blood and Glitter* (I get a mention in there!) and he was the company director for Moscow State Circus, Carters Steam Fair and Psycho Management, and also the co-owner of Circus Extreme, Circus Ukraine and Continental Circus Berlin. Haze came in to *The Big Show* (our name for BBC Radio 2's *Steve Wright in the Afternoon*) with Gerry Cottle in the late '90s, talking about the circus culture in the UK. He was such a supporter of my work, and a genuine, lovely guy.

When the Circus of Horrors performed in Brighton, I met up with him and he told me a scout from *Britain's Got Talent* had come sniffing around. He really couldn't decide whether to accept or not. I persuaded him to go for it, as it would only raise their profile, and after much wrangling over contracts (he wanted to perform original music, which they wouldn't allow) the deal was signed and they appeared on the show. They didn't win, but I think it did raise their profile. I was devastated when Haze died in April 2023. RIP colourful, vibrant man.

Flat sharing in London

Chapter 5
BALLROOM BLITZ

My ticket to performing professionally, and indeed my Equity card, came in the form of my first job as a singer, thankfully without needing to get any kit off. I saw an ad for a band who played weekly in a Mecca Ballroom. This was before the days of what we now think of as clubs, so they were mostly discos and often held in big ballrooms; some even had a house band who popped up for a couple of sets playing covers (imagine suggesting that for a night at the Ministry of Sound!). I got a train to Birmingham to audition and met the soon to become infamous Stuart Brown, who lived and breathed his band, Luna Park. Stuart had big ideas to make it much more than a covers band and was introducing a Space set. He told me excitedly: 'You'll need to wear state-of-the-art silver costumes and sing "Starship Trooper".' No problem, sign me up.

I wasn't a fan of Birmingham. Thankfully I only had to stay there for half the week, then I hotfooted it back to my flat in London, but being in Luna Park was a great experience. We were a disparate bunch of musos and singers in our eight-piece band. The other singer, Lesley, was Stuart's wife – little talent, but looked great rocking the thigh-length boots. Some of the guys in the band had been working with Stuart for years. They were all accomplished musicians who seemed nervous of breaking into anything else, apart from two who most definitely were destined for higher things. The keyboard player Gary Hughes became a dear friend, and I couldn't have been happier for him when he got a gig playing keys for Imagination. I sure was jealous, though: he was touring, doing gigs and earning great money, while I was on a hundred quid a week (actually decent money for three nights' work) but starting to go crazy.

The other guy in the band who went on to greater things, was Mike Stevens. We called him Clever Dick for no other reason than he was so incredibly talented. He joined Luna Park to play sax, but it quickly became clear that he could sing and play keys, guitar, bass and drums. He has had huge success, ending up as the musical director (MD) for such greats as Annie Lennox, Take That, Paul McCartney – and many more!

Just before the guys left Luna Park, we got a great opportunity to come to London to play at the Lyceum for the after-party of the BRIT Awards (I know, right: bonkers!). It seemed so exciting, and we got new shiny daft costumes and practised, practised, practised. Stuart, the band leader, who had long thought of himself as the next big pop star, was beside himself with glee. But it wasn't until we were actually there at the soundcheck, that we realised we would be performing like some dodgy cabaret band in front of some of the original artists. Gary had to brace himself to croak through 'Happy Talk' recently made famous by Captain Sensible, while the actual Captain was shuffling around directly in front of the stage, and one of the most awkward moments of my life was jigging away and singing 'Mickey!'

with Toni Basil literally watching from the dance floor. All I could think was: *Kill me now!*

I had a traumatic experience while working in Birmingham. As it was only three nights a week, I needed temporary accommodation, so I managed to wangle a cheap rental in the form of a room in a shared flat above a church building, a huge five-storey property in the centre with a massive blue neon cross on top. The guys in the band called it The Holy Grail, but I liked living there: it suited me, and there was even a prayer meeting I could go to if time allowed before my gig.

One day I arrived from London at about midday to get settled before the show that night. As I pushed open the door into the entrance hall, I was vaguely aware of a guy behind me, but then, this was a public building, albeit one that was not widely used during the week. I walked into the entrance hall and turned towards the big lift, but something told me, *Don't go in there*. I had started to walk up the stairs instead when he grabbed me, wrapped his arm around my face so I couldn't scream and jostled me back to the entrance porch, throwing me to the floor. I was paralysed with fear. He had managed to lock the front door quickly, ensuring no one would come in. There was no one around, and if there had been, they were five floors above in a huge brick building where no sound would travel. With his hand still over my face, he said: 'Don't make a sound. I'll kill you if you don't let me.'

It's funny: when people talk about near-death experiences, they recall what came to mind. What came to mine was: *I want to say goodbye properly to Mark*. In that split instant when I thought: *This is it*, I felt huge regret that I couldn't see him again.

The guy started to tug at my trousers (I was probably wearing a jumpsuit, which made it harder) when suddenly, out of nowhere, a tall woman I'd never seen before appeared. 'What's going on?' she asked, as the guy fled out of the door, and I lay quivering and shaking with relief. Without much conversation, she led me upstairs and sat me down with a cup of sweet tea, then she called the police, and they took me out in a police car around the city to see if I could recognise him. Of course not, he would be long gone, and he looked like most other dudes wearing jeans and a tracksuit top.

Many years later, I told this story to a journalist for an article in *Spirit and Destiny* magazine, and she said, 'It sounds as though that woman could have been an Angel.' I had never thought of that before. I only know I had never seen her around before, never saw her again, and have no idea how she knew to come and save me.

For a long while after that ordeal, pretty much anything would terrify me, and I no longer walked back to my flat alone. Even in daylight, the guys in the band took it in turns to accompany me, and when I was back in London, flatmates constantly checked on me.

Chapter 6
TOO HAIRY FOR MARI

By Autumn 82, Luna Park was slowly dispersing. As some of the guys were finding their feet, I became desperate to get out of Birmingham and into a proper music gig. I saw an ad for Mari Wilson, she of the beehive hair. I'd seen her sing 'Just What I Always Wanted' on *Top of the Pops* and thought it was a fab song. We had to apply by posting off a CV, a cassette demo and a headshot. I had a half decent photo and demo tape, and I cobbled together a CV. Would it help that I had a BAPA degree? That I had dressed as an orange in an ad campaign for Renault cars? That I'd been singing Hazel O'Conner's 'Will You?' three times a week for months while people slow danced, then gave me rapturous applause in a dodgy nightclub in Birmingham? I didn't know, but to be on the safe side, I included a note that said:

Dear Mari,

PLEASE consider me for this job, I am currently singing in a crap covers band so really need a break with a proper pop band, please save me!

Janey

Mari later told me she had smiled at that and did hope she might rescue me from my dodgy nightclub fate. At my first audition I sang with Jules, or Julia Fordham as she later became known, and after a couple more auditions, we got hired to become the Marionettes – Cinderella (Jules) and Barbarella (me) – in Mari Wilson and the Wilsations. My pop career had begun.

I loved being in that band, an 11-piece, squishing into minibuses and touring all over Europe, staying in dodgy B&Bs and playing just about every university and gig on every circuit in every town. Some of the B&Bs were off-the-scale awful (just as well there was no Tripadvisor then). To cheer ourselves up, we used to mess around. One of our trumpet players, Chris, was ribbed mercilessly for always wanting to get his beauty sleep, so one night they carried his bed out onto the landing. The poor guy woke up and took out his ear plugs and eye mask, only to find he was in the middle of a walkway! Poor Chris definitely came in for some flak in that band. Despite only being in his early twenties, he was almost completely bald, and not the trendiest looking. We played *Sight and Sound in Concert*, televised live from the Hatfield Forum, and our drummer nearly died laughing when Chris stepped forward for his trumpet solo on 'End of the Affair' and a guy down the front shouted (right next to the TV camera): 'F—k off, you bald b—tard!' Live TV, eh?

We also got to do some fun TV shows to promote the records. Notable appearances included Roland Rat (we were all so curious about where the hands went!), a great gig on *Wogan*, and a slot on *The Tube* with Paula Yates and Jools Holland, before flying to Germany, where we were ferried into a TV studio to watch a bunch of totally bonkers variety performers do their mad acts before we mimed to one or two songs and then headed back to the airport. We also got to play all the big music festivals in Europe, being on stage at 1 a.m. in Valencia just before Howard Jones, Strawberry Switchblade and Captain Sensible. I remember hoping he didn't recognise me from Luna Park!

It was 60 quid a week retainer in Mari's band, a bit down on my Mecca band money – but there were weeks where we didn't work at all and I really only had to pay my rent, buy food when I wasn't touring, and keep myself in fabulous '50s dresses (Jules and I would regularly hit Camden and Notting Hill markets) and enough hairspray to make my hair rock. Not quite like Mari's beehive, but big '80s hair none the less.

Talking of hair, as Mari's career progressed and she hit the charts again with 'Cry Me a River', her management company decided the band needed a new image. Well in truth, just us two backing singers. They wanted us to have short bleached 'white' blonde hair, so that we could complement Mari's beehive with a punky look. Now, my hair was long, naturally blonde and really the only bit of me that I liked. I offered to wear a wig, spray in some temporary colour (I tried one strand with green spray and I swear it was still green a year later) – but all to no avail. They said I must 'do it properly'. 'It's only hair,' they added, but deep down I knew it was much more than that.

They gave me an ultimatum, and through my tears, I refused. Then they fired me and got in another backing singer who was willing to cut and dye her hair. The guys in the band were mortified. They felt sorry for me. The only silver lining was a piece in the *Sun* that read 'Too hairy for Mari' with a great pic of me saying that I'd been fired for not cutting my hair but was now in talks for a major record deal. All bollocks of course, but hilarious at the time.

Paul, the drummer in Mari's band, was a dear friend and fairly disgusted that I'd had to leave, so he promised he'd put a word in with some of his contacts who might know of a band needing a backing singer. To pay the rent, I joined another Mecca band – this time closer to home in Dunstable, with a talentless, humourless band leader – and I was miserable. All that kept me going was the other backing singer, a classically trained girl my own age, Janet. We kept each other sane. There was none of the fun and razzmatazz of Luna Park, just a weary bunch of musos, churning out covers for disinterested punters who were only out on the pull. Paul rang me regularly and said: 'Don't crawl round the carpet with Harry –' (his expression for letting depression get the better of you) – 'something will turn up'.

Turn up, it did. Just as I was watching *Top of the Pops* one night, on came Wham!.

Chapter 7
CLUB FANTASTIC

No one can deny the way Wham! rocked that *TOTP* stage, and I loved them instantly. Halfway through their song, the phone rang, and it was Paul saying: 'See those kids on the telly? A mate of mine has been asked to put a tour together for them, no idea if they need a backing singer, but here's his number…'

Jake Duncan was the surly Scottish tour manager who had landed the job of managing the first tour for the new hit sensation Wham!. He was happy to hear from me, as a mate of Paul's, but he said it had little to do with him. 'Come down to Nomis Studios,' he said. 'The band's MD Tommy Eyre is seeing lots of musicians and singers, so it's worth a shot.' I rocked up at Nomis – so named because it's 'Simon' backwards and owned by Simon Napier Bell, who became Wham!'s manager. I knew the studios well, as lots of bands rehearsed there. Tommy Eyre was immediately friendly and invited me to stand and watch while a few musicians played some riffs, and he jammed around on the keys. After they had left, he played a few chords and asked me to try some harmonies. Fortunately, I'd learned a few Wham! songs and then he played a new one, and was impressed how quickly I picked it up. 'Problem is,' he told me, 'George and Andy have been advised to get a vocal section (singers who already work together and are used to harmonising). I've got Kokomo coming in soon. I think that's what they're looking for.' Kokomo were an established and pretty hot US section who sang on lots of hits. I thought quickly. 'I *am* part of a vocal section,' I said, 'I work with a guy and a girl.' His eyes lit up. 'Really?' he asked. 'Great, bring them down, have a jam, I'll get George and Andy to have a listen.'

Back home, I frantically flicked through my address book. Of course I wasn't really part of a vocal section, but I sure as hell was going to form one that night. I asked Janet first; just like me, she needed a break from being in a Mecca band. She was beside herself with excitement and said, 'Let's rehearse'. First, I had to find a guy, though, so I contacted Gee Bello; I had sung with him on some vocal sessions for adverts. He had been in the pop/soul band Light of The World and I wasn't sure if they were still touring, but when I rang him, he was excited too and said one tour would be no problem. We literally knocked up some harmonies over the phone – God knows how! We agreed on our story that we'd been doing sessions together for months. I rang Tommy Eyre back and arranged a time for us to pop by the studios.

We arrived as George was rehearsing with the newly formed band, and he beckoned us to take the mics and jam along. Afterwards, he brought Andrew Ridgeley in to meet us, and the rest is history. Seems they did want a ready-made vocal section but were happy that we were 'young… fresh'. We got the gig! Eat your heart out, Kokomo.

* * *

The first Wham! tour, Club Fantastic, was literally chaotic. We played theatres and relatively small concert halls. After a few weeks' rehearsal we headed off to our first gig, two nights at Aberdeen Capitol Theatre. Up until we arrived at the soundcheck, they hadn't told us what we were wearing on stage, which for such an image-conscious band seemed odd. 'You'll get your costumes when you arrive' was all manager Jake Duncan would tell us. We'd heard rumours that the guys had done a promotional deal with FILA sportswear, so you can only imagine how much Janet and I were dreading it. Sure enough, we arrived at the theatre to find the biggest boxes you'd ever seen filling the stage, and the guys flinging T-shirts and shorts around wildly, laughing at how ridiculous they were going to look. Dion Estus, our gorgeous enigmatic bass player and a big guy with long dreads, took one look at the tiny red short shorts and said, 'I ain't wearing that shit!' The guitarist, Hugh Burns, was a session player but not known for either his height or his sense of flamboyant clothing. Somehow, they got him wearing the shorts. He almost drowned inside them. Someone must have had a word 'cos Dion rocked them too.

Janet and I had to get to work and fast. The FILA polo tops were awful. I mean, Airtex is great for playing basketball, but we wanted to be young and glamorous! We cut the sleeves off, turned them into vest tops and then set to work on the shorts. They were awful boys' sports shorts, so it was impossible to look like anything other than a netball teacher in them, but Janet got handy with a needle and thread and we made them much shorter, took the sides up and captured it with a ribbon so they looked a bit more funky. To add insult to injury, the dancers Shirlie and Pepsi got to wear four different gorgeous costumes for their appearances. One of the funniest moments was George and Andy trying on Shirlie and Pepsi's white frilly dresses backstage. If only we'd had smartphones! We were so jealous, but we knew our place.

We got over ourselves…eventually. No one cared, the audience had come to see the boys, and after the warm-up from DJ Gary Crowley and a dance act called Eklypse, George and Andy rocked the red and yellow kit onto that stage – and brought the house down. Had it not already been down, it was full collapse when George did his shuttlecock stunt… pulling it from his shorts and throwing it into the crowd. It was such a shock we found it hard to continue singing. I'm not sure any of the band knew he was going to do that!

I don't think any of us, apart from perhaps the huge security team hired to protect us all, had expected the scenes with the baying fans. I'd seen footage about Beatlemania and I can only imagine this was what it was like. George and Andy left the stage at least 10 minutes before the gig ended, without saying goodbye, and we continued playing while they got straight into a Black Maria waiting behind the backstage area for a quick getaway. Once we came off stage and got changed, we expected to walk calmly to the tour bus or our chauffeur-driven cars, but no, we too were hounded, fans clawing at the bus and dangerously trying to hold back its progress, as if by being close to us, they could get a piece of George and Andy.

Other fans were such fun, though, waiting outside the hotel to try to catch a glimpse of the boys – who were just lovely and spent time signing autographs, etc. The tour merchandise included dolls, one of George and one of Andy. George was always miffed that Andy's doll sold out faster. It was the one item of merchandise that I couldn't get; they simply sold out at every gig.

We really were one big happy family on that first tour, all travelling together and staying in the same hotels. Of course, George and Andy would have pseudonyms to avoid fans being able to ring or find their rooms, and Andy took great pleasure in calling himself by as many bizarre names as possible: 'Mr Creosote' was my favourite. He used that for a good long run, before the fans found out and started ringing the reception and asking to be put through to Mr Creosote.

The drummer, Trevor, used to bring his girlfriend along; George's friends Pat and Dave, were also usually with us, and sometimes George and Andy's parents. We nicknamed them the Royal Family. Andy's mum, Jenny, used to give us all a royal wave, which was hilarious. I found a cutting of a piece in the *Sun*, with the headline 'Mums on tour'. It relayed that 'Heartthrobs George and Andy' were being chaperoned by their parents. Wham!'s publicist Connie Filippello always toured with us, as did the managers, either Simon Napier Bell or Jazz Summers and his girlfriend Yazz (yes, she of 'The Only Way Is Up' fame). Melanie and Yioda, George's older sisters, came on all the tours in the UK. Yioda helped with costumes and Melanie was a top hair and make-up artist. I was very grateful for her (finally I got to work in a band where it was OK to have big hair!) and even when tours ended, I'd go over to their parent's house in Radlett and Melanie would cut and style my hair.

Spending small fortunes on his hair was a thing for George. He would regularly fly Mel out to wherever we were, and sometimes, while we stayed in a fairly basic hotel in the US, George would fly back on Concorde to get his hair done. Another *Sun* story reported Tommy Eyre complaining that while spending thousands on his highlights, George and Andy gave band members only a souvenir programme and a T-shirt worth £3 at the end of the tour. I'll never know if Tommy sold his story to the paper, but I don't agree they weren't generous. I was very happy with the money we got and never felt exploited. Their generosity extended to guest tickets too. I became very popular with friends all over the UK who wanted to come to the gigs, and even managed to invite my mum and dad when we played Bournemouth International Centre (BIC). At the after-party George was charming to them, and my parents, having barely been out of their home in years, were suddenly

My beloved Famous Names t-shirt

living the high life, mixing with celebs, because, of course, lots of other musicians wanted to come and see Wham! We were in (a rejuvenated) Birmingham at the same time as Kool & the Gang and Thin Lizzy and if I remember rightly, they all rocked up to the gig and the after-party.

It wasn't easy coming down after the shows, and you can absolutely see why so many musicians drink themselves half to death. At that point, I couldn't really hold my beer – a glass of wine and I was done – but sometimes I'd go to the hotel bar with the guys (Tommy liked a drink) and nurse an Irish coffee. I remember one night in Newcastle where Ozzy Ozbourne kept us all entertained till about 4 a.m. Who knows whether he actually did bite a bat's head off, but I think he believed he had!

With all the action of being in such a huge pop group like Wham!, I barely got time to take stock, but sometimes I thought about how quickly things had changed. I remember thinking, *WOW, this is it, I've arrived!* Here I was doing all the things I'd dreamed of doing as that child back in Stapleford watching ABBA on TV: I was making money and having so much fun just doing what came naturally to me – singing and showing off!

When tours come to an end, it's always a massive anticlimax. We'd all hug and cry and wave goodbye, not knowing if we were going to see each other again. In fact, the core backing band barely changed in all the tours, apart from a change of backing singer. Gee left and was replaced by Leroy, and the brass section changed around a bit, but for the most part we were a unit and became a bit of a family. I recently came across a tour programme from their second tour, The Big Tour, and we'd all signed each other's programmes. There were such lovely messages written on mine, lots of in-jokes that I won't bore you with, and it made me remember how close we were. But now, it was back to real life, at least until the next Wham! tour, and at home, things weren't going so well.

Chapter 8
WEATHERING THE STORM

I'd met Ray on the rebound after Mark and I split up for good. I had just finished college. He was a tall, quiet, fairly shy blonde sound engineer with a Christian band who got chatting to me at a festival in Cornwall, and the brutal truth is I loved him, but as a friend rather than the love of my life. *Ouch*… the truth hurts, and I didn't face it till many years later. The reality, I think, is that at some unconscious level I longed for a father figure and he quite enjoyed that role and seemed to want to live – vicariously through me – an exciting life. Ours became an agreeable relationship for a good few years, but something in me always held back. Deep down, I must have known that, like Mark, this wasn't forever. One or two of my close friends concluded that too. I knew I didn't want to get married or have kids, and thankfully, Ray didn't mention that either.

As time passed, he became quite controlling, and I am so ashamed that I didn't deal with that better. I remember a friend, Steve Taylor, suspecting that not all was well with Ray and I, wanted to duff Ray up in the car park one night when he found out about one particular incident. Luckily (and with Steve being about half of Ray's height) that never happened. I was never physically hurt, but the emotional gaslighting (as it would now be called) was off the scale. I became quite insecure and fearful; the only silver lining was that it kept me thin. I remember one of George's girlfriends telling me one day she thought I was so pretty, 'glowing', and I was incredulous, I could see that she wasn't just stroking my ego, she really meant it. I simply couldn't accept that I was even OK, let alone worthy of the accolade of being attractive. Ray had often put me down in terms of talent too, so I lost confidence, to the extent that I was terrified of being found out. Terrified that someone might say, *Hold on, there are much better singers than you, you shouldn't be doing this top league work!* I now realise that pretty much every professional suffers from imposter syndrome – that inner critic who tells them they are totally not worthy of their own success.

Looking back, I realise I had very low self-esteem. Despite knowing deep down that it was time to leave, I didn't think I deserved better. I stayed far too long. There were however, some good times among the bad with Ray. He was surely a Jekyll and Hyde type: sometimes he was lovely. I just didn't ever know which identity he'd present with, which always kept me on edge. When I say I stayed far too long, I mean 14 years. If you're reading this and you know it's time for you to leave a relationship, reach out for some support. You deserve to get free.

Chapter 9
EUROVISION DREAMS

When the first Wham! tour ended, I had no idea when and if I'd get the next call, so life had to go on. I constantly auditioned and chased my tail, and one day I saw an ad for a singer in a band being put together for a contest to decide the UK's entry into the Eurovision Song Contest.

Back then, *A Song for Europe* was a big thing. Ten songs chosen from hundreds were performed live on TV and the audience then selected their favourite to represent the UK. I got the Tube to the audition, and there in front of me stood a couple of the band members from Brotherhood of Man, Martin Lee and newest member Barry Upton along with Tony Hiller who had apparently worked with them for years. Barry was just a couple of years older than me, and despite the fact that I wasn't especially a fan of Brotherhood of Man's cheesy music, the track they'd penned for Eurovision wasn't bad. They chose me to be one of the band, called us Rubic (terrible name) and shoved me with another singer, Janet (not Wham!'s Janet) who could not have been more different to me, and a sax player called Sean. Our track was called 'When The Kissing Stops'.

What ensued was a whirlwind of costume choosing (*SO* many arguments and I hated what we ended up with – bright pink shirts, black miniskirts with trousers and a black tie) and lots of rehearsals with choreographers who did their best to make it all gel. We performed at the BBC Television Theatre as part of a live show hosted by Terry Wogan, and I was ridiculously nervous. We lost, but a few very good things came out of the whole experience. One, I dated Barry for a while. He was a self-assured guy, yet another tall blonde (though this one looked more like Barry Manilow). He was a real gentleman and helped find my feet, encouraging me to buy my first car, a little yellow mini for £20. (I actually left Ray for a time, and am incredulous now that I went back!) Barry and I to this day remain good

Rubic – A Song for Europe Eurovision Entry

friends. He was and will always be a total pop tart and I love him for it. He went on to write several pop hits (think Steps and Sonia.) I also got to meet and become friends with the lovely Carrie Grant, who had auditioned at the same time for another band, Sweet Dreams. Their song 'I'm Never Giving Up', won the British round and they went on to represent the UK in the Eurovision song contest. They lost, but what an experience for Carrie! She is such a fabulously talented singer and went on to meet and marry David Grant (she's heard all the gags about Carrie Grant!), the two of them working together as TV voice coaches, and now radio presenters and authors. The following year, as if one *Song for Europe* experience wasn't enough, I went back for more.

This time, the management really seemed to know what they were doing. Razzamatazz management, fronted by Jill Shirley, were the force behind Bucks Fizz, so they knew their pop music. The band were Belle and the Devotions, Belle being one Kit Rolfe, and she needed a couple of singers either side of her, in a Supremes kind of way. I loved their track 'Love Games', which had a '60s feel and really suited my voice. I signed their contract, we started looking at costumes, and it felt exciting – until one of the management team booked me an appointment at a leading hair salon. I actually think it was Trevor Sorbie, and to this day I wish I'd reminded him of this on the many occasions he came into Radio 2. She deposited me into his salon and said words to the effect of *Do your magic on her, darling.* Thankfully, Trevor considered it as merely a consultation and explained that he'd been briefed that as backup singers we needed to complement Kit's bleached white hair, by having bright red hair (the other singer) and short chicken yellow hair (me). That was the look they were going for. *OMG – was this really happening to me again?* I laughed at first – a one-off gig, appearing on TV, which might go no further. Surely, I could wear a kooky wig? Sadly not. 'It's only hair,' The woman from the management company said, (I'd heard that before!) before she waltzed off to buy more designer clothes while Trevor explained the process. 'We'd have to start by completely bleaching your hair. Take out the natural colour, then dye it bright yellow.' 'Will I ever get back to my natural blonde?' I asked. His look said it all; I suspect he thought it was a terrible idea too. The contract was ripped up, and I was fired again before I'd even started! They won *Song for Europe*. I sat watching the show and sobbing at what I'd missed out on. The song was actually great, and they went on to represent Britain but then lost – and, in fact, got booed for some reason. That didn't bring me any pleasure; I was happy for them. They did, however, disappear as fast as they'd arrived, so thank God I didn't chicken-yellow up for that three minutes of fame.

Another gig that I thought might be hidden in the closet forever was the bizarre experience of touring as a real-life Barbie doll! Luckily, since the release of *Barbie* in 2023, even my teenage daughter thinks it's cool! It was one of the first *Pop Idol* type events. Rowley Fletcher, a marketing agency in London, had Mattel toys as a client and they wanted a full-on tour to promote their new doll, Rock Star Barbie, and her band: Dee Dee, Dana and Derek. Annie Rowley, the CEO who later became a great friend, apparently hired Pineapple dance studios in London and had queues of wannabe singers and dancers queuing round the block for days! They cast the gig, held a massive launch at the Hippodrome, hired a songwriter to produce an album's worth of material, and set about getting costumes made that were exact replicas of the dolls. They knew the press would pick up on it, and around that time they discovered that the girl they'd chosen as Barbie had got her kit off at some point. As already mentioned, dancing topless was a popular choice among my peers to get an Equity card, so she was hardly Slut of the Decade, but the management simply couldn't take the risk of putting their client in jeopardy, and the contract stated that Barbie must be 'squeaky clean'.

They needed a new Barbie, and fast, one who could slot into the role – dance, sing and wear the same costumes – and it just so happened that the producer of the music was Paul Ridgeley (yep, Andrew's brother) and he recommended me. Within a few days we were rehearsing and then into the minibus for a hilarious tour of theatres and kids' venues. Mostly they were afternoon shows to hordes of screaming kids and their nonplussed parents. There was usually a toy shop or department store strategically nearby and we'd all schlep along after the show to sign copies of the dolls.

The costumes really were something else. I had the biggest, heaviest, longest blonde curly wig ever; thick, pink Lycra tights; silver, high-heeled cowboy boots, a white PVC miniskirt, silver top and pink jacket; oh, and a huge pink bow in my hair! This was a full-on show, so we had a costume change where I had exactly two minutes to get out of that lot and into a meringue-style, pearly white ball gown for the show ballads. On one leg of the tour, I got the management to hire my best friend Alison to come along for the ride and help me into my kit! There was a mirrorball on stage, too.

One of our gigs was at the Hippodrome, very bizarre; I can't remember quite how that one came about, but also on the bill that night was Angie Bowie. She made a beeline for me in the dressing room, and made some interesting suggestions by the sink… I politely declined. Clearly, I wasn't rock 'n' roll enough.

When the whole of the UK turned Barbie-tastic for Margot Robbie, I posted a few of my Barbie pics on Facebook. One woman commented: 'I took my daughter and her cousin to see you in this show. They're both 43 now but I bet they still remember the "beautiful Barbie girl".'

That makes me feel older than God.

Rock Star Barbie on Stage

Chapter 10
THE BIG TOUR

It's funny to think that for all their incredible legacy, Wham! didn't do many tours. The first Club Fantastic Tour in 1983 – with those first gigs in Aberdeen, then rocking through Edinburgh, Glasgow and a whole host of UK theatres – had been a huge success. I remember the Lyceum in London: although a fantastic gig, it was a bizarre experience for me because I'd played there with Luna Park. Towards the end of that tour, George had throat issues, diagnosed later as polyps on the throat, and we had to postpone a couple of dates. I recall Andrew saying that he never felt George loved touring the way he did. He preferred his home life, but if that's the case, it didn't show on stage.

We were all aware that George and Andy were becoming increasingly unhappy with their contract with Innervision Records. And, of course, their old Bushey contact had given them their first break, but being so keen to sign, they hadn't exactly gone through the small print in detail. Jazz Summers and Simon Napier Bell managed to extricate them from the deal, and sign them to Epic Records, but meanwhile Innervision weren't disappearing quietly. Around that time, we appeared on the Channel 4 show *The Tube*. I was beyond excited to be doing the show again. *The Tube* was live, and as the opening chords to 'Good Times' started up (the only cover we did on the live shows), George used the eight-bar intro to tell the fans NOT to buy the new 'Club Fantastic Megamix' that had been released by Innervision. Contractually, there was nothing Wham! could do, but they were determined that their fans knew they weren't pleased. I called my parents from a phone box after the show, and my dad was incredulous. 'Did that boy tell his fans *not* to buy his album? You'll be out of a bloody job if they carry on doing that!'

Meanwhile, the press was having a field day with George and Andy. During one tour, we saw an exclusive spread where a couple of *Sun* Page Three girls claimed to have been proposed to by Andy. They did a terrible Photoshopped pic (probably scissors in those days) showing the girls either side of Andrew, each claiming they'd been given a ring. Much hilarity, alongside frustration, ensued. I remember us girls talking about it with Andrew in the dressing room. He'd never even met them!

With the *Make it Big* album, Wham! seemed to move into a different league. Tracks like 'Freedom' really showed George's development as a songwriter. He was happiest in the studio, and while Tommy Eyre and a few of the band got to join him on some recording sessions, none of the backing singers were ever invited. Not because he used different session singers, but because he sang all his own backing vocals (BVs). He would spend hours harmonising, tracking and tweaking. He just didn't need us unless it was live, when obviously he could sing only one part. We did get to be part of the live video recording for 'Everything She Wants'. Such a fun day, and the resulting bit of black and white film is still one of my favourite memories. 'Everything She Wants' was the B-side to 'Last Christmas', which stayed in the charts for 13 weeks, one of the biggest selling singles not to reach Number 1 – until 2023 that is!

Wham!'s popularity was flying high and in the winter of '84, we were in rehearsals for The Big Tour. We were to kick off in the UK, then on to Japan, Hong Kong, Australia and the US. This time, George and Andy travelled separately from us. They never seemed distant, though; we really were still one big family and we all stayed in the same hotels – thankfully, no more dodgy three stars; we'd made it and the hotels reflected that. I remember one of the gigs on the UK leg of that arena tour at the end of November at Whitley Bay ice rink. I've no idea how they transform an ice rink into a theatre, but clearly it involves covering the ice. Sadly, it's still totally freezing, and I recall arriving at the soundcheck to see a group of our roadies literally trying to thaw out a couple of teenage girls who had managed to hide overnight in the venue to ensure a good place near the stage. Our lovely roadies gave them hot chocolate and a telling-off but made sure they warmed up right by the front barrier.

That Christmas was a big one for Wham!. 'Last Christmas' came out on the same day as 'Do They Know It's Christmas?', so they decided to donate royalties to the cause. The Band Aid track sold millions and it must have been bittersweet for George and Andy as they made only Number 2 in the charts. The tour included a staggering run of nights at Wembley Arena at Christmas time. I have such fond memories of singing the backing vocals to 'Last Christmas' with the fake snow twinkling down around us.

After a break over the new year, we flew to Tokyo for the start of the Japan leg. I lost a lot of weight during the dates in Japan: for a vegetarian there was almost nothing to eat. The guys in the band were delighted to be invited to special dinners with geisha girls, unlimited saki and Wagyu beef. 'They massage the cow,' the guys would tell me, but all I ended up eating was a thin soup, that had a film of oil across it – and that 'rainbow soup' was pretty much it for two weeks. Everything about Japan was so vibrant and exciting: we did all the touristy stuff, visited lots of pagodas and gardens, went on the Bullet train, and Tommy Eyre and I went to the theatre to see a traditional Japanese Noh drama, an experience for sure! Western pop music was massive at that time in Japan, and the fans were enthralled by us all. It was a bit sad, though, to see that lots of the young Japanese girls had tried to die their glossy jet-black hair blonde to look like western pop stars. Sadly the effect was slightly dried, ginger locks with black roots, so they looked more like bedraggled tomcats.

One night, I woke up to find the bed shaking – and sure I hadn't had that much to drink! When the lamp collapsed, and a picture slid off the wall, I realised that either I was having some kind of poltergeist experience, or this was an earthquake. In the hotel and all public buildings, I had seen lots of warnings about earthquakes, and what to do in the case of an emergency, but I wasn't expecting to actually experience one. Panicking, I rang Janet's room. By then a bunch of our band were out in the hotel corridor in their PJs, wondering whether we would need to evacuate or not. Our tour manager went to reception to get the lowdown, where apparently all was total calm. It was a very tiny earthquake, nothing to them. They'd been through far worse.

The next stop after Japan was Australia (where this memoir began) and I remember that both Janet and I were so desperate for a healthy meal that we begged the coach driver en route to the hotel from the airport, to drop us off at the nearest eatery. He pulled up alongside some shops and we jumped off the bus, telling the tour manager we'd get a cab to the hotel. We literally ran into the nearest place, which happened to be a Pizza Hut, and devoured the salad bar as if we hadn't eaten in weeks. We took The Land of Plenty by storm, and then it was onto the USA. I'd never been before, and I loved my first trip, especially to New York. We stayed near Tribeca and visited the Apollo Theater in Harlem. George had been asked to sing alongside some greats on their 50th birthday celebrations. During the soundcheck, a few of us got to pose on that stage where all the legends have played. It was very special.

That first US tour saw us playing small venues and staying in fairly low-budget hotels. We hit San Francisco, checked into a terrible hotel and within about 20 minutes all checked out again. It brought back memories of the Mari Wilson days! Fortunately, when the management had made a mistake like that, they were very good at repairing it quickly: they checked us all into a four-star with a rooftop pool, and supplied limousines to take us to clubs if we wanted to go. We were all asked to be part of the recording for 'The Edge of Heaven' in a New York studio too, and while there, several stars popped by to say hello. The most memorable was Brooke Shields, who was so friendly. We got on really well and I felt as though I'd known her for years. It was just after that when I realised (if I hadn't before) that you really cannot believe everything you read in the British press: 'George Michael's new love Brooke Shields is to star in the video for his new single,' said the headline. 'Love struck Brooke (20) was at George's side as he recorded last week.' What BS! She dropped in, met everyone and we shared a tuna mayo bap. It made a great story, though, and added some glitz and sass to George's image. In reality we never saw him with girls, other than his friends. Andy, as you can imagine, was often seen with a glamorous girl in tow, but George seemed much too focused on his music. I think if you'd asked the band about George's sexuality, there may have been the odd joke, but in truth, we just didn't know, and really, it didn't seem to matter.

Our first trip to LA was memorable too. For some odd reason, we were booked into another awful motel in the Franklin area. It felt very dodgy, like the one in *Psycho*. George and Andy were away doing promo – or maybe getting highlights or nose jobs, depending on which rumours you believe – so after a couple of nights when we heard gunshots firing and all got a bit concerned, (despite having our own room, Janet and I shared because we felt scared) Tommy Eyre spoke up on behalf of the whole backing band, complained and got us the hell out of there – to Miami, in fact, for a quick holiday before the next gig. Living the dream!

At the end of The Big Tour, there was a party in London at Legends, and it was hard to get through the crowds of paparazzi to get in. The invitation said: 'End of The Big Tour party', to celebrate three months of hard graft around the world. It wasn't hard graft, really. I think there were literally a million gals my age who'd have swapped places with me! Some of the US parties were legendary. How I wish I'd kept a diary: one was at a famous actor's home where there were Picassos on the walls, the Dom Perignon flowed and I was introduced to so many famous faces, I lost track.

Generally, Wham! liked throwing parties, and in addition to the many parties on tours organised by promoters, record companies *et al.*, they arranged a few back home. Sometimes we would all go to the restaurant in Edgware owned by George's dad, where Jack (real name Kyriacos) Panayiotou held court and served us hungry musicians endless courses, alongside demonstrating what a work ethic really means! It was fantastic fun, and the ouzo flowed.

There was a big party at a stately home in Hertfordshire too – for one of George's birthdays, I think. It was palatial, and the very first time I'd ever since an ice sculpture. I'd read about such things but couldn't believe how cool it was to be up close to a thing of such beauty! Amid this absolute glitz and glamour, Andrew swanned in, long tartan designer coat flapping. He breezed up to a group of us who were chatting to George, and said: 'Hi and bye, can't stay long, gotta go to a party.' I think a driver was always waiting with the engine revved, in case he got a better offer.

Chapter 11
WHAM! IN CHINA

It wasn't long after The Big Tour ended that I got the news that we would be playing China. I'm not sure any of us realised quite what a big deal it was. I've since learned that George hounded Simon Napier Bell to get them something huge, to get them a gig that would set them apart, and no other Western band had ever played China. It wasn't that easy. Originally no one was open to the idea – all too political – but Simon persisted. George too was relentless and wouldn't give in. It's hard to believe now that it all happened before the changes. There were tourists on guided trips to the Great Wall of course, but there we were, a huge entourage complete with film crew, rocking up an absolute storm to audiences who had never experienced anything like it.

Our tour guide for the trip was a lovely guy called Ching. He spoke excellent English and managed everything for us, travelling with us on the coach trips and sharing all the history. He organised some kind of 'state dinner', where we were treated like royalty and offered strange, exotic meats, and a rare delicacy, 100-year-old eggs. We passed – well, apart from Andrew, who was always game. Andrew also had to give a speech to eminent dignitaries, and we were all trying to help him write that on the bus.

A trip to the Great Wall was mandatory, of course, and we took some great pics of us all wearing the ubiquitous dark green caps with a red star. We were escorted on visits to temples and other attractions, and it was all filmed. A huge crew headed up by film director Lindsay Anderson of *O Lucky Man!* and *Look Back in Anger* fame, followed us around to film what was to become a full-length feature. But despite some exotic footage in the Chinese wet markets (oops… that has different connotations after 2020) and some unique concert scenes where our DJ, Gary Crowley, rocked the stage, and the audience, who had previously had experience only of classical concerts, clapped politely, slightly out of time – something went wrong. George and Andy reportedly didn't like the rushes and even though

Official Wham! in China hat

George flew his sister Melanie out to sort his hair, things didn't seem to gel – no pun intended.

Lindsay and crew left, and the footage ended up as a sell-through video, *Wham! in China*. I enjoyed it, though. I still have my copy and occasionally show my teenagers. *That's Mum bobbing about on stage and chatting* (via hand signals) *to a Chinese theatre worker backstage.*

The Chinese audience, at least at first and perhaps because of their government's influence, seemed very wary of us. Our first gig was at the Workers' Gymnasium in Beijing, and the most bizarre experience. Behind the seated, very subdued audience was an actual line of police officers, and when a few students at the back started dancing, they were told to sit down again, and a scuffle broke out. We later heard they had their ID cards taken from them (their ticket to everything). It was very disconcerting for the band, and couldn't have been more different to our usual rocking gigs with screaming fans and total mayhem. We learned that the ticket price for the Wham! shows were equivalent to three months' wages, impossible for the average person. There were some lucky chambermaids in our hotel who got some freebies from us! Everything really was all about money. It seemed almost impossible for the crew to get permission to film any footage, till they got the hang of offering sterling (Chinese money or US dollars wouldn't do).

The Canton gig was better, and more exuberant, and while George didn't seem to care much about anything other than composing, recording and singing great music, and having huge critical acclaim with chart hits, the trip served its purpose: it set Wham! apart as a cultural phenomenon and paved the way for other British bands to play there. The press at home was non-stop, and *Smash Hits* ran a huge spread covering the whole trip. I guess they must have had a journalist and photographer as part of our entourage; it was hard to say, as we were one huge group!

When we finally left China, Tommy suggested we have a whip-round and collect some cash as a gift for Ching, our tour guide. We amassed a tidy sum and Tommy presented it to him, but he was horrified! 'Thank you,' he said, quite emotional, 'I am not allowed to accept gifts or money.' One of the guys asked if could accept goods if they were used, and he said he guessed so. The next few hours saw the whole entourage digging up their expensive perfumes, toiletries, skincare and make-up to give to Ching. Some of us had bought duty-free items, so we simply ripped off the packaging and added it to the pile. He left with a huge stash of goodies that I like to think he treasured, but what a state of affairs, that an intelligent well educated and well-spoken guy couldn't accept a gift! He looked very downcast when we said, 'You must come and visit us in England!' We really meant it, but he wasn't allowed to leave, of course. It made us all sad and very grateful for our freedom.

During our trip in China, I had my second near-death experience. We were flying from Beijing to Canton and one of our brass players had been acting very strangely for a few days, not emerging from his room. The *Sun* reported that he had been asking for an exorcist and 'the whole band were gripped by a fear that he had been possessed by the devil.' Please God! I never did find out the full story, but it seems he had tried to get into the cockpit, which of course did not go down well. The *Sun* also reported: 'There was blood everywhere'. There wasn't. The plane nosedived, lost pressure and the masks flew down from the carriage above our heads. I remember turning to Janet and saying: 'If this is it, thanks for being a good friend', but as we fumbled with our masks and reached for the life jackets under the seat, the plane lurched back upwards and everyone calmed down. Our gentle giant security guards had done a manoeuvre (safely) on the brass player, and all was well. He was flown home soon after and not much more was said, but I doubt there is anyone on that flight who doesn't remember how scary it was.

From China we ferried to Hong Kong, and that was yet another shock to the system. The guys in the band were like kids in a candy store, buying every conceivable gadget and having suits made because Tommy had found a brilliant tailor who could knock up a suit in the finest silk in a few days for a fraction of the cost it would be at home. I didn't fancy a suit, which seemed a bit too Annie Lennox for me, but I did buy several metres of blue silk and somehow fitted it into the suitcase. I have no idea where it ended up. We all wasted so much money! I must have bought at least five kimonos in Japan, and another bunch in Hong Kong, and as for trinkets and gifts, it's incredible we didn't end up paying airport tax.

* * *

Wham! was not a continuous income for me, and back home, I never stopped looking for work. I didn't have an agent, so everything was literally word of mouth – and sadly, despite being able to sight-sing, I just wasn't in the inner echelon of session singers who got all the work on adverts and TV music. I did a few cool jobs, though, including singing on an ad for Harmony Hair colour. 'I'm Huh, huh, harmony… Do you dream in colour? … What colours do you dream?' See, I can remember it even now! I got paid a reasonable amount for the session, which was in a little recording studio in Carnaby Street, but what I hadn't factored in was the repeat fees. I ended up earning about £10K from that one little session! I did a session or two with Barry Blue, he of '70s fame, and sang on an album for Billy J. Kramer (for which I never did get the invoice paid, Billy!).

I sang backing vocals on a weird and wonderful gig for a bunch of big-time guitarists at Wembley. I'd barely heard of Albert Lee, but it seems he is deified among guitar players. There was also a session I did for a well-known singer who will remain nameless: he was absolutely vile, drunk, out of his head on cocaine and rude to everyone in the studio. I sang my backing vocals, warded off his advances while reeling from his whisky breath, and legged it from the studio. I did get paid, though, and a little over the agreed amount; I think his manager was embarrassed. Years later, watching *The Boat That Rocked*, I realised that the stereotype pop star image really had been true back then. Mostly, I wanted to keep busy, and being a singer in a big pop group was great leverage for getting gigs. It got me out of the house too, as things were at a kind of stalemate with Ray. Fortunately, back into my life came Wham!

Chapter 12
WHAMAMERICA!

The huge North American Tour kicked off in the autumn of 1985. This was their opportunity to really make it big in the US. It was never a given that UK bands would succeed there, but Wham! certainly did.

We filled huge arenas and stadiums, with support acts of such high calibre it caused quite a stir. We did one gig with Chaka Khan as support, another with the Pointer Sisters, and many other bands I'm embarrassed to say I've forgotten. Lots of celebs came to our US gigs too. Andy was beside himself with excitement when the Bee Gees rocked up (*Saturday Night Fever* had been his teenage thing) and I'd wager he still talks about the night Jimmy Page came backstage with his daughter. Andrew, a mega fan, was embarrassed for Jimmy that he had been dragged along by a teenage girl! Rumours went around (excuse the pun) that Stevie Nicks came to our Hollywood Park gig but got turned away by the security guards… *ouch!* I will always remember seeing Elton John at the side of the stage at one of our gigs in the US, and later going out for dinner with George. He knew talent when he saw it.

Getting to tour the States again really was amazing. I hated Houston, Texas (way too hot for me) but I loved Chicago. I'd been connected with a photographer friend of the guy I'd met in Sydney. 'You must meet up with Gregg,' he said. 'I'm sure he will do some cool pics for you.' I called him, invited him to the Wham! gig, and we met up for dinner.

Gregg Eisman was one talented photographer, that much was clear from the off. His work seemed to consist of incredibly artistic black and white shots of nude models in fencing gear (a very good look!) and some dark film noir type pieces. He invited me over to his studio, and it was honestly like being in a film: think *Desperately Seeking Susan*. His apartment was a huge, converted warehouse, so incredibly stylish, long before the East End of London had heard of warehouse loft conversions. 'I'd love to take some photos of you,' he said, 'complimentary, of course.' I suppose I was thinking of the kind of promotional headshots I'd had done when I was modelling, but he had no such ideas. 'Let's get creative,' he said, 'we'll hit the thrift stores.' We drove to some charity shops, and he picked up a totally scruffy, lacy white wedding dress. 'That's it,' he said. 'We'll use that'. I don't think I understood the avant-garde at the time, and I had no idea why I'd want to pose in a wedding dress, but I was a bit in awe of him, so I played along. We drove to a rubbish dump ('recycling centre' we'd call it now) and climbed over the gate, then he held his coat around me (though there was no one around – thankfully) while I changed into the wedding dress, which he'd ripped even further. 'Sit and look forlorn,' he commanded, which wasn't hard, being perched on a pile of detritus. He handed me a cigarette to top off the look! We then drove down to the shores of the lake, and he took some fantastic shots of me in the water, the train of the dress trailing in the sea. In the dusk light it looked very odd, and some tourists stopped to ask why my dress was so damaged. Wide-eyed, they asked where the groom might be. I LOVED those pics. I loved Gregg, and we hung out for a week or so. Although there was a small part of both of us that might have wanted it, the spark of romance just wasn't there.

Despite the tour being called Whamamerica! it included Canada. Being in Toronto was a whirlwind, and that was the only date across all the years when we had a security issue. We all went on stage at the Toronto C.N.E and when we came back to the dressing rooms for the interval, lots of us found we'd had personal belongings stolen. Whoever the thief was got one hell of a haul: we'd just been paid our PDs (per diem expenses) for the coming week, ouch! Thank God we didn't have passports, etc. with us, and were mostly wearing any expensive jewellery on stage or it was back at our hotel. The tour insurance sorted it, but it was not the best experience for my first time in Canada. Janet and I did get to go out of town, though, to visit her relatives, who had a lakefront cabin by the forest, like something out of a film. They collected us from the hotel on a day off, drove us out there, made an incredible barbecue (Janet and I were both still veggie, but she had a hot dog anyway if I recall!), then drove us back to the city.

We had our own warm-up acts on that tour, in addition to the major artists who appeared with us. Just before Wham! came on, the crowd were whipped to a frenzy by a couple of dancers, Dennis Elcock and Danny John-Jules. Danny was later famous for playing Cat in Sci-fi comedy *Red Dwarf*, and I loved his sense of humour. Between

A photoshoot on a rubbish tip in Chicago!

… and midnight by a lake in Chicago

Wham tours, we met up in London, when I went to see him doing his thing on roller skates, in the first-ever cast of *Starlight Express* on the West End stage in 1984

Meanwhile, I don't think there were any of us on that tour who weren't catching a glimpse of George as a massive solo superstar. He didn't talk about it – to us anyway – but we were in the early stages of witnessing the emergence of George Michael as an artist in his own right. With each performance, his charisma, talent and stage presence shone brighter, and it became increasingly evident that George was outgrowing the band and on the way to becoming a singer/songwriter with boundless potential.

WHAMAMERICA! before doors open

Chapter 13

THE GIGS THAT WERE, AND THE TOUR THAT WASN'T

You'd have thought that because Janet and I had done the entire Wham! tours we'd be in great demand as backing singers, or at least individually for sessions, but sadly it didn't work quite that way. I think lots of people assumed we were full-time: I was often told, *I'd have called to offer you the gig, but assumed you were on tour with Wham!*. It was quite frustrating having to hustle to get gigs. Janet deep-dived into operatic stuff, and became very successful in musical theatre, but I was still locked to pop music.

For about five minutes, I got really excited that I might actually hit popstar fame and fortune myself because some session work turned up for the Hit Factory. Pete Waterman, Matt Aitkin and Mike Stock were churning out so many pop hits at that time, and I became determined to get Pete to do something with me. We lunched, but clearly I just wasn't quite what they wanted. I did, however, get to sing vocals for a Sam Fox track and backing vocals on 'Toy Boy' for Sinitta. It was on that session in South London that I heard a highly amusing Paul Young story. The producer went to make tea and offered me the last chocolate digestive. I popped the wrapper in the bin, and he shouted: 'No! We have to save the wrappers for Paul Young, he saves them for the coupons. You get money off next time.' Filthy Rich and desperate for 10p off his biscuits! To this day I call collecting money-off vouchers 'doing a Paul Young'.

I got an opportunity in the late '80s to work with Kim Wilde, and honestly, they were some of the most fun gigs I've ever done. All over Europe, they loved Kim. We all did, she was totally gorgeous and the whole tour was a family affair, with her dad and brother, Marty and Ricky Wilde, often travelling with us. I remember one tour when her parents didn't come, though, and Kim was a bit badly behaved according to the tour manager. For the life of me I can't remember what had happened, but she was having a bit of a sulk and didn't want to come out of the hotel room to do promotional interviews.

The tour manager called her mum in despair and held the phone out for a few of us to hear as Joyce shouted: 'Knock on that hotel room door, tell her to get out and do as she's told, or I will come over and slap her arse!'

We flew out to MIDEM, a big music biz conference in Cannes, and I was amazed to find that we were on the bill with James Brown! That was something else! I was doing backing vocals with Julia Fordham again and my strongest memory was that her bag had been lost at the airport, so she was stressing out. Some of my make-up was in there, so I was too, to be honest. We were on stage saying hello to James Brown at the soundcheck (bowing down actually) when the tour manager burst in holding Julia's bag, which had arrived from the airport: Ta-da! All adoration of James Brown was forgotten, the bag all she cared about! It's been wonderful to see how Jules' career has panned out: at the time of writing she lives in LA and is still recording albums and touring with a few other legendary female singers such as Beverley Craven and Judie Tzuke.

After Kim's tour I got a gig with Nik Kershaw when he was relaunching with a new album *Radio Musicola*. Again, he was huge across Europe, and we did lots of trips to Germany, Denmark, Paris and Spain for just one TV show or a slot at a festival. I was singing with a talented guy called Steve Lee, who was also an amazing musician and writer, and Nik's wife, Sheri. That wasn't the most comfortable of vocal sections. I couldn't help but have the impression that Sheri thought any other women (there were just the two of us in the entourage) were after her husband, so I felt constantly under surveillance. It didn't go down well when the European fans were showing their appreciation for Nik, who was still a teen heartthrob despite being in his thirties. I reckon Nik's manager used to pray that she wouldn't insist on doing the live TV interviews with him, for fear of what she might say!

I was booked to do a huge world tour for about three months with Nik's band and set about getting a dep in to cover my duo singing work (another singer who would stand in so that I could keep the gig till I returned). I found someone who was grateful for the work, cancelled anything else in the diary and all was all set. Rumours stated to fly that the tour may not be happening, or was it that our drummer had broken his arm? I never did find out, but suddenly we were told the tour was off. We were dropped just like that, and I never saw any of them again (apart from Steve, who became a great friend). I asked about getting paid anyway because I'd depped out my own work, but was told, *No, there's nothing to cover that.* Something told me: *That can't be right, these big tours all have watertight insurance*, and indeed there must have been a very genuine reason to cancel a world tour. We weren't told, but I decided to seek some advice. I was recommended a top music biz lawyer who said he would take the case on – no win, no fee – and so it began. To start with, Nik's management ignored us completely, then we got a one-line response saying there was no money. The lawyer said: 'Be patient, let's write to them again,' and while this was going on, Steve called me and said, 'Did you get your repeat fees for the Roland Rat TV performance?'

I hadn't received a cheque or any notification, so I contacted the ITV payments department, and they confirmed that a cheque was issued to me and sent via Nik Kershaw's management. Interesting! The lawyer investigated and found that they had cashed it in. The lawyer suggested that we might have a potential fraud case on our hands. Of course, there could have been a perfectly legitimate explanation, and they were about to issue payment, but it seemed worth the lawyer enquiring about that too. He suggested to them that they might want to settle the tour payment in full as well as the outstanding TV payment, and then we wouldn't need to take it further. Lo and behold, a decent-sized cheque arrived not long after. Even with the lawyer's cut, I was grateful, but as a general rule I avoid conflict like the plague.

Chapter 14
THE FINAL

I've already said that as a backing singer, or in any capacity in the music biz, you can never be sure of the next gig, and so it came to be that when Wham! announced The Final at Wembley I didn't get the call. I can't deny that even now, I feel sick to my stomach. I didn't ever get a reason. Lots of the band had changed, and they hired a bunch of established session singers and new brass players, and I don't know if it was because I wasn't right now, or simply that I wasn't in the frame. A long time had passed, George had done a fair bit of solo stuff and was moving in different circles, and I just wasn't considered. To add insult to injury, Kim Wilde's band was one of the support acts and they didn't call me either!

Crawling around the floor with Harry (*see* Chapter 6) was most definitely on the cards then: I was working covers gigs, a few sessions and writing my own stuff, but aside from a few ads I wasn't doing anything especially lucrative or exciting. Talk about feeling inadequate, and not enough. It didn't matter that I'd done the entire run of Wham! tours and TV shows and worked with lots of other bands, I just became convinced at that point that I was worthless. I felt rejected, and my mantra became: *Nobody loves me, nobody wants me, I think I'll go and eat worms*. I was invited as a VIP guest to The Final, and to lick my wounds I went along, and had a great time bopping along to all the hits I'd been singing, next to lots of celebs and stars who were seated in the VIP area. I'm glad I saw it. I didn't see George again till he came into BBC Radio 2 to be interviewed years later. It wasn't awkward, though he didn't say 'sorry' for not hiring me for The Final. (Just kidding!)

Chapter 15
CHASING RAINBOWS

Naturally, I still needed an income. I was signed on with a few agencies, which led to some acting and modelling gigs. One favourite was a job on TV with Robbie Coltrane where the big man did an impression of Robert Palmer, singing 'Addicted to Love' complete with iconic backing band. I was one of those women musicians with short black hair and black minidress. They did a pretty realistic job. I stood behind the keyboard in my short black dress – and my hair? Amazingly they didn't ask me to cut it – guess that would have been a bridge too far for a day's work – and they managed to make it magically disappear under a slicked back dark wig. I got the TV bug and signed up with lots of extras' agencies and was lucky enough to get some fantastic jobs. Just as Ricky Gervais's *Extras* show reveals, there is a heck of a lot of downtime hanging around on film sets, but the company is usually good and the food is fantastic. On the *EastEnders* set they used to call the extras 'The Hoovers', 'cos they'd come in and hoover up all the food from the catering vans.

Some of the notable jobs across that period included being a dodgy prostitute in *The Bill* (who wasn't in that programme in the '80s?). I went to Southampton a few times to be in *Jemima Shore Investigates*, I was in some crowd scenes in big films including *Batman*, and some wonderful historical dramas filmed at mansions. I remember filming for a Lew Grade film at Luton Hoo, the stunning stately home in Bedfordshire. We had to arrive at 4.45 a.m. for hair and make-up, and then be squeezed into nightmare corsets under massive dresses with a bustle. Once I was strapped into my pale blue silk contraption, I was convinced no one would notice if I loosened off the ties of my corset to enable

Addicted to Love

me to breathe even slightly, but the costume gal came running across the set to hoist me back in. God, were those costumes uncomfortable! The film was *A Ghost in Monte Carlo* with Joanna Lumley, Sarah Miles and Oliver Reed, to name just a few of the stellar cast.

My dance training came in useful for a grand Viennese waltz scene in a huge ballroom, and I was picked to partner Oliver Reed. He was charming, but totally sozzled at 10 a.m., so revolving round the room with me when his head was spinning wasn't the easiest for him.

Another film called *King Ralph* starred John Goodman as the long-lost wayward relative who finds himself appointed King when the Royal Family mysteriously go missing. Best of all, I got to choreograph John and a handful of dancers doing a routine to 'Duke of Earl'. I just happened to be hanging around when they realised they needed some

On the set for *A Ghost in Monte Carlo*

dance moves, and lo and behold, my degree came in useful again!

During this time, I met and became great friends with the lovely Sarah Cracknell (of Saint Etienne) and then her dad, Derek, who, rather handily was a big-time first assistant director on lots of films, including *A Clockwork Orange* and *Batman*. That really helped in getting more work, and Derek was great at teaching us to keep our head down if we wanted a long run of extra work: being featured, or even speaking a line, may feel exciting and earn you a bit more, but that's you off the film, in case you're spotted again in the crowd!

Keeping it in the family, Julie Samuel, Derek's wife and Sarah's mum, soon became pivotal in my career. Julie had been a successful actress in her time, and was moving into music management, working with Mick Bund and the band Felt. She encouraged me to record my own single and together we came up with the surname Lee Grace. I changed it formally by deed poll and have never looked back.

Julie's friend was photographer Joe Bangay, an old-style Fleet Street photographer who was a sucker for a Page Three girl type of pic but had a heart of gold. After telling him a thousand times: *No, I won't be posing topless, however tasteful,* Joe took some great headshots, and we found a couple of producers and brought out a track called 'Heartbeat Radio'. It was an OK record, and made it onto Radio 1 *Newsbeat*, but without the weight of a big record company, it didn't do more than skim the lower end of the charts.

Somehow, Julie managed to connect me with the DJ Paul Oakenfold, and we collaborated on a cover of the Donna Summer track 'Love to Love You Baby'. We worked with Graham Stack, who later wrote for Take That, Tina Turner and more, and we created a funky version which did well in the dance chart. The record label paid for a plugger, and we were all set to get some plays on Radio 1, but just as they requested more copies, the record company's MD went off skiing and the moment was lost. This was quite a common occurrence: I had colleagues in bands whose track had been about to get some airplay on Radio 1 which could have shot them into the charts, but something newsworthy

Publicity shot for Heartbeat Radio

happened, and that was that. It's all about timing. To promo that track, Julie and I (Paul was already Big Time too busy) toured around the UK to local radio stations, and that's where I got my taste of just how much fun it might be working in a radio studio. Typically, I'd go in and be interviewed, chat about the Wham! days, etc., and on one occasion – I think it was BBC Radio Leeds – the presenter asked me if I'd stick around to read out a few letters or some such. I loved it! A little lightbulb came on as I realised this was something I could do – you know, 'read out loud' – so an idea started to form. I wanted to work in radio. I had no idea how to go about it: I knew hospital radio was a way in, but that didn't feel quite right.

I clearly remember the day I heard an ad on Greater London Radio GLR (now BBC London) saying: 'Would you like to learn some skills to work in radio? [Gimme!] Are you under 21 and living in Vauxhall? If so, apply now.' Ah, so excited for 10 seconds before being let down. But I took note of the address and wrote a letter:

> *Dear Sir or Madam,*
>
> *I am a regular listener to GLR and heard your ad on the Emma Freud show. I would love to apply to learn some skills to work in radio. I have a degree in performance arts and have been working in the music business for several years as well as the film industry. I have enclosed my CV. However, recently I have realised that I would love to work in radio and my dream would be to work at GLR!*
>
> *There is one problem, I am a little over 21 and I live just outside of London in Herts, rather than Vauxhall but I would challenge the BBC on being 'Age-ist' and 'Area-ist',*

surely it should be equal opportunities for all, despite age and location?

I am joking!!! Of course, I understand that you need to fulfil requirements for funding for training, so if this course isn't possible for me, could I A) pay for it myself, or B) could you recommend somewhere else I could get some similar training to equip me to work in radio?

Yours faithfully,
Janey Lee Grace

A few days later, I got a phone call. 'Is that the very cheeky Janey Lee Grace?' said a strong Caribbean accent with an obvious amusement. 'Yes,' I said cautiously. He continued, 'My name is Syd Burke, and I am running the training programme for the BBC in Vauxhall, I like your style! Well done you for challenging us, your passion is obvious, come and do the course. Let's not mention the area you live, just be on time, we start at 9 a.m.' I was ecstatic! Syd Burke was another very important catalyst for change in my life.

Those three weeks of training in Vauxhall were exhausting and exhilarating. We spent some of the time at Grafton House BBC training facility in London, and some of our time out and about recording vox pops and the like, but mostly we were learning production skills, presentation skills, scriptwriting for radio and, of course, editing – splicing actual recording tape with a razor blade! We had to produce packages, whole programmes and trailers; it was comprehensive and all complementary. I had literally fallen on my feet. I found such a passion in it all and asked Syd: 'What do I do now?'. 'Volunteer', he said. 'Go to GLR and offer to answer the phones or make tea.' So off I went to

Marylebone High Street and spoke to Trevor Dann. I think I got an audience because he was impressed I'd sung with Wham!. He said, 'I'll keep your number, but we don't really need any phone operatives at the moment.' As he started to walk away, he turned and said, 'There is one thing. One of our weekend presenters is struggling for help, I don't suppose you know anything about Christian or gospel music, do you?' He said it with such disdain, I hardly dared tell him that yes, it was my world, I'd been a Greenbelt Christian festival regular since I was a teenager and I knew an awful lot about Contemporary Christian and gospel music; in fact, I was an actual fan. He looked surprised. 'OK, well, I will introduce you, I'm sure you can help produce some of the features, give her a hand.'

Three or four weeks later, after doing bits and pieces to help her out, *The Gospel Hour* presenter left and I was offered the show. It was 7 a.m. on Sunday morning and I had completely free rein to produce and present – for peanuts money, but what experience! I can't say I felt I'd earned the gig because of my presentation skills. Trevor's words to me were: 'Quite honestly, no one else wants it!', but hey ho, that show was my ticket into the world of radio, and I loved it.

With the help of Ray (who loved doing showbiz tech stuff – editing interviews and the like), I made it much more than the sum of its parts. I occasionally pre-recorded my shows and would leave the tapes (actual reels of tape in those days) for the engineer to play out. They put the fear of God into me about correct labelling on the boxes, because another radio station apparently had an engineer whose job it was to play out a recorded documentary at Easter time. The tape reels were not clearly marked, and the doc aired, playing the story of the Resurrection *before* the Crucifixion! By then I'd made friends with one of GLR's most charismatic characters, producer Chris Whatmough, who jacked up (radio lingo for scheduling) guests for the mainstream shows such as Richard Skinner and, later, Chris Evans. Producer Chris would often ask the pluggers bringing in the artists if they'd spare 10 minutes for a recorded interview with me, so I got to chat gospel music with Bobby Womack, Candi Staton, Gloria Gaynor and many more greats. The show won an award and even Danny Baker, whose show followed mine, sometimes acquiesced that it was 'not too bad, some of that Christian stuff', though he thought I was stretching it playing Van the Man 'just because he includes the word "God" in some of his songs'.

Chris Whatmough became such a wonderful friend and supporter. He loved the glitz and glamour of the music biz and the fact that I'd toured with Wham!, and when the Paul Oakenfold track charted in the dance charts, I honestly think he was more excited than I was!

He proudly introduced me to everyone in radio and music, so despite being just a small-time presenter of a one-hour show on GLR, I knew all the presenters, pluggers and lots of the bands and artists. I recall when Chris Evans first arrived at GLR, fresh from Newcastle, I'd just been to a photo session for *Smash Hits*, so was pretty glammed up, and Chris introduced me as the Gorgeous Janey. Chris Evans winked and said, 'We could be married within the hour, you know!' He was, and is to this day, so charming and genuine.

Years later I remember hearing the news that Chris Whatmough had died. I was heartbroken. I miss him and still think of him, pretty much daily. RIP.

Around that time, I got a chance to work in commercial radio. Radio Essex offered me a very badly paid, two-hour show on a Saturday. It was a very different experience, 'jocking' and playing in advertisements, but it really helped me cut my teeth for taking live callers on air and finding something to say when quite frankly there wasn't much. The combination of the experience of working with both the BBC and independent radio would stand me in good stead later.

I was still pitching out for sessions and getting the odd bit of work or short tour. I teamed up with my old Wham!

Going solo at the Mean Fiddler

bandmate Janet, in the band I-Level – 'Let's dance again in a minefield', remember that line? We toured with Osibisa and did a few club gigs and festivals with other bands. I can't honestly say that was my world: there was a LOT of 'substances' flying about and I felt a bit insecure. Together Janet and I also toured as backing singers with Patsy Kensit's band. I could at this point be mean, and say Patsy wasn't the best singer, but in fairness she said it herself. In fact, we met her at the rehearsal rooms, when she was only 17 and very fresh-faced, and she said: 'Please can you guys sing the main vocals alongside me, because my voice is very thin and flat!'

She was managed by Muff Winwood, and they actually were great pop songs, but poor Patsy, wearing a black bikini top and floppy hat in a seedy club, never felt quite right. She'd be nervous introducing the songs, and some smart alec near the front of the stage would shout: 'Oh yeah? Who's gonna sing that one, then?' Clearly pop stardom was not to be her path, and as soon as the film *Absolute Beginners* was released, it was obvious the pop career would always come second to acting for Patsy.

Sometimes I'd be called up as a backing singer for the odd TV show. I sang with Natalie Cole and the Womacks, and Janet and I did a few TV shows with Matt Bianco. I remember that with fondness because they'd given us no indication of what to wear (déjà vu from the early Wham! days). We rocked up at the TV studio for the Saturday morning show in our usual look – black miniskirt, lacey tops, fringes, *etc.* – and the manager said: 'Mmm, it's not quite right, I'll have to go out and find something for you to wear.' We gave him our dress size, and literally bit our nails through the rehearsals wondering what he would come back with. We couldn't believe it: he rocked back in with funky white and beige patterned chino-style trousers and really funky vest tops with a slogan, and they looked great. Neither of us would ever have chosen those clothes, but they were spot on.

I was also working hard to write my own songs. I don't know if I was ever much good, but I had some great collaborators. To earn cash, I was working with a piano player in a duo set-up. We played in wine bars, at weddings, functions, etc., did all the covers of the day and a bunch of classics, and when we needed a bigger band, we augmented with a drummer, sax player and guitarist.

Some of the working men's clubs we played at were dodgy, to say the least. Most had bingo as their main attraction, and there were gigs where we had to end a set early because the football was coming on the telly, which was in the same room. I even recall trying to sing to a few small children on the dance floor while their parents watched the TV positioned above the stage! One club in South London had a strict policy around volume, and a traffic light system installed. It's not as though we were Van Halen, but on one occasion the light shifted to amber, and everyone panicked that a notch up on the PA and the whole power would cut! There were some real horror stories from those clubs. I heard of a band having to pack up their gear during a wedding reception while a full-scale fight was going on, the best man and the groom throwing punches at each other before the whole room, including the bride, joined in. Apparently, they still got paid!

Talking of punch-ups, Steve Taylor (who had earlier offered to duff up Ray) was our drummer, and a writer, and he inspired me to write my own songs. 'Let's just do it,' he said, and forced me to come up with some lyrics. Before long, we had a bunch of songs that weren't bad, and we put a band together (after advertising in the *Melody Maker*, of course). The most fun was playing the Marquee in London: we felt like a proper rock band, despite the fact that the club was only half-full. Hey ho.

Around the same time, I was also answering ads myself in *Melody Maker*, searching for the elusive partnership. I also used to look at the noticeboard in the music shops in Denmark Street in London, and it was there I saw an ad saying: 'Singer wanted for electro pop band for recording.' I rang up and a friendly guy called Nick answered the phone and invited me to come for an audition in Walthamstow. I arrived, and it was just his lovely Greek aunt to welcome me, then Nick arrived and said, 'My writing and recording partner Phil will be here soon.' I glanced out of the window and coming down the lane was Johnny Rotten – well, it sure looked like that. Phil was a bizarre combination of goth and punk, but the sweetest guy ever. He is also the most talented piano player I have ever met, and I've met a lot. We did some tracks as a three-piece, and then Phil and I started to write songs together. That partnership had a great energy, and we did some fun gigs including the Mean Fiddler and a tour of the UK and Ireland with a charity show. We did some Christian gigs too, and it felt as though everything was coming full circle after my gospel show.

* * *

At the end of the '80s, I was loving doing my GLR show as well as a few singing sessions, but the touring had mostly dried up. I continued to pitch out to bands and producers, and to do some extras work whenever Derek got me a gig on a film. I also did some promotion work when times were lean. I hated that, in truth. One gig was walking around at Earls Court Exhibition Centre in a Bunny girl outfit, pretending to find it highly amusing when, one after the other, hideous drunk businessmen fluffed my tail and made a flirtatious comment. Thank God, things have changed; they'd never get away with asking young women to do that gig now. Most actors still find themselves needing to supplement their income with that kind of work, though. Just recently an actor shared a hilarious story of how she was having an anxiety attack (well, that bit's not funny) when working for a company with a promotion on hot dogs and having to run down the street crying and wailing, dressed as a sausage. The things we endure for our art!

Out of the blue, I got an opportunity to work with Boy George. By this time, he had his own record label and was co-writing with a fantastically talented guitarist called John Themis. I got to do a few appearances and sessions with George and hang out with him and John. Until I saw him at work, I don't think I had realised just how talented George is. Of course, we know and love his voice, but he is also a brilliant songwriter. Sometime after that, George along with Jeremy Healy – he of the dreadlocks and 'John Wayne is Big Leggy' fame – formed their own dance label, More Protein. He had a few great acts, including MC Kinky and Eve Gallagher, and I sang backing vocals on their tracks and popped up on PAs at some London clubs. I also spent many hours hanging out with Jeremy Healy in his flat in Camden. The idea was that we'd write some tracks, but somehow in the haze of a smokey room (not guilty, Your Honour) nothing got achieved. [Years later, I bumped into George at a West End show. I was in the bar and, for some reason, my old mum was with me, but he came straight over and said, 'I know you... backing singer… Janey with the yellow hair.' My mum, who really missed her vocation as a mouthy stand-up retorted, 'While we're talking colours, I'm not sure about that lipstick on you, duck!' He didn't seem to mind.]

I was, of course, battling on with the 'trying to be a pop star' bit. Keyboard player Phil and I continued to write and play gigs around London. Sometimes, it was to a couple of people and a dog, at venues like the Mean Fiddler in Harlesden, but we loved it. I recorded some tracks with the fabulously talented Kipper (real name Mark Eldridge), who became well known working with Sting. At that time, he had a band called One Nation, and he turned out to be another clever Dick – literally a brilliant singer, guitarist, writer and producer. He introduced me to a woman called simply 'She', who had a bunch of Cyndi Lauper-style compositions. I worked with Kipper to demo a few and they pitched out to some record companies. Who knows why I wasn't signed!

Chapter 16
FROM THE REAL WORLD TO POP ROCKET!

It must have been the late '80s when I was really crawling the carpet. I had some covers gigs to bring in money, but very few sessions and didn't seem to be getting the tours anymore. I loved doing my GLR radio show, but it was peanuts money, so I decided I might need to get a real job.

I had absolutely no idea where to start but was volunteering with a local family whose daughter had muscular dystrophy. I had been feeling sorry for myself, and Ray, rather wisely, had said: 'The best way to shake yourself out of it is to do something for someone else', so I found a befriending agency, jumped through a thousand hoops to show I was trustworthy, and started to visit a lovely girl called Susan. She was in a wheelchair, had little or no mobility and limited speech, but she could feel and she could smile. I used to force myself to manage her huge unwieldy wheelchair, and we'd go to the local church, where for an hour or two she could move a little finger to the music and be made a fuss of having tea and cake afterwards. I found it excruciating: the services were mostly boring, I had nothing in common with anyone, but boy, did it do me good. Seeing Susan's eyes light up for a short time meant everything and shook me out of my entitled, dopamine-seeking self for a while.

Thinking of it now reminds me of the wonderful line from Kae Tempest's poem 'Brand New Ancients'. They describe Gloria, the barmaid in the pub, and the line is: 'If she smiles at you for a second, it'll last you all week'. That's what it felt like, being able to make Susan happy just for a moment. Above all, it made me realise just how impossible life was for Susan's mother. There was just the two of them, so she was her daughter's sole carer, and while she literally never complained, she did explain to me that she hadn't slept properly in years: she had to be alert and listening for Susan's breathing patterns, as irregularities could be fatal. If anyone caught a cold, it could be life-threatening for Susan, and her mum was a walking ball of anxiety.

I'd never before considered just how difficult the life of a full-time carer could be, and so when I saw a part-time job offered for an admin/promotion's assistant for a Carers Association charity, I decided to go for it. Because of my experience with Susan, and my obvious enthusiasm, I got the job, and it was eye-opening: *People pay you for rocking up to an office, answering the phone, typing some emails, sending some letters off? Plus, you get sick pay and holidays? Wow!* This was all new to me having been self-employed since leaving college. There wasn't a huge amount to do, truth be told, so to earn my keep I set about putting on an exhibition at the local library to raise awareness of the plight of carers in the UK. It was a huge success, we got lots of press coverage and had a reception with the mayor attending.

It was the day after the exhibition launched that I was offered a session for Saint Etienne. My friend Sarah Cracknell had found fame with the band, and she now recommended me for a side project involving band members Bob and Pete. It was a day I wasn't working, so off I drove to Surrey to work with producer Ian Catt on a track they wanted to try out in the clubs. Bob and Pete were always incredibly creative, and along with Ian loved including clips of film noir in their tracks and experimenting with whatever was going to be next in the dance scene. I will always remember that it took me just over 2 hours to get to that studio session from Hertfordshire, and 2 hours to get back, and that the actual session lasted 55 minutes.

All you need to do, Ian said, is sing: '"7 Ways to Love", just vamp it.'

'What about the rest of the lyrics?' I asked. 'Is there a lead vocal?' 'That *is* the lead vocal,' he said, 'just those four words, and a bit of ad-libbing with some oohs and ahs.' OK. Job done, £80, thank you.

Bob and Pete finished the track, did a 12-inch (vinyl) version and got some acetates pressed to give to DJs they knew to try out in the clubs. The idea was that if the track was a floor filler it would be worth releasing, so it was just an experiment. Rumour has it – and I genuinely don't know if this was a fabulous PR stunt – that a DJ in Scotland (where the rave scene was huge) saw that it was indeed an instant floor filler, bootlegged 500 copies of the track and sold them out of the back of his car.

Literally a couple of weeks later a rather stunned Bob and Pete called me to ask, 'Are you OK to front this track, as it's your voice? We have a whole bunch of record labels with their cheque books open, but they want to know who the band is.' I said *yes, of course*, and found myself in a photographic studio with one of Bob's old mates Andrew Midgely, a keyboard player who'd had nothing to do with the track, but he'd do. We were an unlikely couple, had absolutely nothing in common, but who cared?

Julie Samuel became our manager, and within seven weeks of signing to Arista Records '7 Ways to Love' shot to Number 8 in the charts. It was Number 1 in all the dance charts too. I'd never seen the music industry move so fast! Exactly nine weeks since I'd started my part-time job, I had to hand in my notice. The other staff awarded me the prize for the most unique excuse for leaving: 'I have to free up time to be on *Top of the Pops.*'

It was true! Suddenly I was in demand. We were rushed from one photographic studio to another, we were wanted for radio interviews, print interviews and an appearance on *The Hitman and Her* with Pete Waterman and Michaela Strachan (remember that show?).

Rocking my *Avengers* look

Appearing on *TOTP* was a dream come true. I'd wanted to be on that show since I was a teenager, yet for some reason it never happened, either with Mari Wilson (she did 'Cry Me A River' solo) or Wham! (they just had Pepsi and Shirlie dancing), and the other guys I was working with didn't have big hits around that time, so to get to do it in my own right was amazing. And yet, ungrateful snob that I am, I was suitably miffed that it was a *throw it against the wall and see if it sticks* track where I sang literally four words over and over again.

But it stuck, and I now look back and regret not stopping to enjoy that time a little more. OK, so I wasn't exactly a respected singer-songwriter, but the rave scene was huge, and somehow, we managed to be cool. Alongside the articles in *Smash Hits* and the dance mags, we were featured in *NME*, and taken sort of seriously. It was also, in fairness, a banging track, and still sounds great on the dance floor all these years on.

The upcoming *Top of the Pops* appearance meant finding something to wear and some dancers to make us look good. The last bit was easy: we hired a couple of gorgeous gals, called them 'The bunnies' and they choreographed a great routine and gave me a few simpler moves to do alongside them. Sadly, that was not to be: in my desperation to find the right outfit, I simply couldn't factor in being able to move. The record company got me a stylist because we had a photo shoot the day before the TV show. I had a long conversation with her about my preferred style. 'I like to look a bit '60s,' I said, 'I love black, fringy stuff, flares, silver spangly outfits, glamorous kinda clothes, ya know, funky. I like most things in Hyper Hyper' (the huge market-style fashion emporium in Kensington).

'I've got it,' she said, 'I'll bring along a whole host of outfits for a photo session, then you can pick one out and wear it for *Top of the Pops* too,' which was scheduled for the following day. Having never been much good at shopping, other than trawling charity shops, I was super-excited to see what this cutting-edge fashion stylist would gather for me.

I couldn't believe it when I arrived at the trendy warehouse studio in Shoreditch. She rolled in late, wheeled in a small suitcase and then, with all the panache of a magician pulling a rabbit out of a hat, revealed her suggestions for my outfit: a knee-length tartan kilt and a roll-neck jumper. There may have been an ill-fitting mustard coloured shift dress in the collection too. I kid you not. She was gushing about how 'on trend' I'd look and after hours of putting it off by spending way too long with the make-up artist and hairdresser (who did the most awesome job, thank God) we started the shoot. The stylist must have decided I was definitely not on trend enough for her, and got bored remarkably quickly. She mumbled something about needing to shoot off to see a show, and could we be sure to bring the outfits to the TV studio?

As soon as she'd gone, the lovely photographer said to me: 'You're not at all comfortable in that kit, are you? Want to try a few wearing my biker jacket?' *Now you're talking*: all the best shots were in his leather jacket. Thank you, God.

Of course, that left the problem of what to wear on *TOTP* and only a few hours before rehearsal to find something. Julie and I scoured Hyper Hyper and Top Shop, found some funky minidresses and wigs for my dancers, but nothing for me. I'd worn my flared trousers on other shows, so wanted something different, but time was running out.

In the last hour before we were needed at the studio Julie said, 'Let's hop in a cab to the East End, there are some cool vintage shops.' It was there I saw it: the perfect vintage '60s minidress, silver and sparkly and complete with porthole. It was perfect but on the tight side. I could get it on, but if I moved, even slightly, everyone would be in for an eyeful.

Anyone watching that *TOTP* clip will see I am demurely keeping my legs together, not a dance move in sight sadly. Worth it for the frock, though. I also managed to lay my hands on a glockenspiel used in marching bands; it was the funkiest thing, and perfect for the 'middle eight' bit of the track. Of course, I had no idea what I was miming on the glockenspiel, much to the hilarity of my classically trained friend Alison, but I think I got away with it!

They'll hate me for sharing the story, but on the night of *Top of the Pops*, apparently Bob and Pete rocked up to the studios and weren't allowed in. Oh, the indignity. We were the front guys! They did, however, make most of the money as writers, so I guess they got the last laugh.

We also needed a pop video – and quick. We had a meeting at Arista's office to discuss what kind of video it would be, and very soon realised that they wanted something fairly low-budget but had literally zero ideas. The meeting was dragging on, and they were getting nowhere until I tentatively asked: 'Could we somehow play on the number 7? Take the old Magpie theme: one for sorrow, two for joy, three for a girl and four for a boy, five for silver, six for gold, seven for a secret never to be told.' I mean, come on, it was a brilliant idea! There was a murmuring around the table, and the meeting ended. There was no *Hey, great idea, Janey!* They literally never acknowledged me, but just got to work making it happen.

We filmed in a warehouse with a cardboard cut-out of Andy and one of me (wish I'd been able to keep that!) and a couple of Chinese actors who played the 'girl and the boy'. It was cheap, simple, but very effective, and then someone had the idea, and I'm so grateful to them, of making the end scene one of me riding a moped singing the lead line. I simply sat on the moped with a funky helmet, against a green screen, fluttered my false eyelashes and mimed. It was a funky video and worked beautifully.

In 2022 my son was at university doing Media Studies. One of his modules involved critiquing and analysing pop videos. They were given a list of about 20 'iconic' pop videos to study, and he called me, laughing, to say our '7 Ways To Love' video was one them! Of course, he didn't choose that – can't own up to having a mum in a '90s rave band! He does occasionally, however, tell me that he did use it as a flex sometimes: having a mum who had a '90s hit that some of his mates still found themselves dancing to in the clubs, was sort of cool.

Then came the requests for the PAs (personal appearances), and it was literally the best way to be clubbing in the early '90s. We got to swan in, have a few drinks, do a 10-minute set and sign a few records. Julie would collect a couple of thousand quid, and we'd be off.

One gig was supporting Deee-Lite at Brixton Academy. The soundcheck dragged on for hours, and Andrew popped out to get some food. It was literally five minutes before we were due on stage when Julie's phone rang: poor Andrew had been outside the stage door for a full hour arguing with security guards who simply didn't believe he was in the band and wouldn't let him in!

On another PA, our support act was a bunch of spotty youths called Take That. They were not exactly 'polished', but such fun and you could literally see them learning on the job. Their manager, Martin, would troll them round, force them to rehearse, then watch like a hawk as they perfected their cheesy dance moves and charmed the girls. The gorgeous one, Mark Owen, asked for an autograph from Andrew and me. Years later, when they came into Radio 2 to be interviewed, I didn't mention it.

You'd think I would have made a lot of money doing those gigs, but the reality is all the costs came off the top. The manager takes 20 per cent off the fee. Then there are the travelling expenses (no public transport ever worked because we were typically on stage at 2 a.m.), food, hotels etc., any props, tech stuff, then we had to pay the dancers, and often someone to help us on the night if Julie couldn't make it. What was left was split between Andrew and me, and usually we got less than the manager. Hey ho.

Talking of expenses, Julie decided after a couple of months to ask the record company if she could see the accounts. We were all a bit green, but it sure was revealing. Obviously, the cost of the video, photographers, cabs to studios, etc. were listed clearly, but what we hadn't been expecting to see on our expense account (i.e. before we got paid any royalties) was about £400 for bouquets of flowers for the dressing rooms at *TOTP*! And the huge bill for entertaining us at a local bistro afterwards. How naïve of us to think that was at the record company's expense!

The only thing we managed to get knocked down from the expenses list was a staggering £12K bill which had been paid to something listed as 'Spotty Dog'. Julie was like a spotty Rottweiler herself when she rang them up about that one. 'We have most definitely not taken purchase of a dog, spotty or otherwise, so what is this for?' It turns out that the record label, without discussing it with us at all, had decided to hire a rapper (said Spotty Dog) to produce a rap version of the track. It went straight in the dumper. You can see how big artists feel they're fleeced. When my dear friend Martyn Joseph was signed to Sony, he played a small Christian festival in Harrogate. Sony sent him there in a private helicopter, much to the amusement of the grubby, soaking, not too easily impressed campers. Imagine Martyn's dismay when he realised they'd charged him thousands for the privilege, and it would have been only two hours on the train.

* * *

With the chart success of '7 Ways to Love' you'd think we'd be able to crack another hit, but sadly all Bob and Pete had up their sleeve was a rather subdued track 'He is Cola'. We tried to make something of it, but it bombed and Arista dropped us like hot potatoes. There was an extended version of the track, though, so it came in useful for our PAs.

I still shiver when I remember one PA in Newcastle: it was on a party boat by the dock, and we were being paid a decent whack. Julie and I set off from London and Andrew was arriving by train, aiming to arrive just before the gig. On the way up, stuck in traffic on the A1, I was idly rifling through the paperwork, checking the time we were needed on stage, and to my horror I saw that the contract said: 'minimum 20-minute set'. 'We've only got about 12 minutes if we're lucky with "7 Ways to Love" and "He is Cola", even the 12-inch versions,' I told Julie, with some horror.

'Ah, don't worry, it will be fine, I'm sure that happens all the time,' she replied, ever laid-back.

But I'd done plenty of clubs with my duo hat on, where they wanted every ounce for their two-penneth and I was

Janey with Cola Boy manager Julie Samuel

very nervous of taking the risk. 'What options do you have?' Julie asked. We could hardly start doing a version of 'Heartbeat Radio' or a Wham! track. I remembered that Andrew had said he had 'been working on some stuff' and knew it would be a 'dancey instrumental' track of some sort, so I quickly rang him on the mobile. 'Yeh,' he said (also laid-back), 'it's about 10 minutes, just some riffs and chords and stuff, quite spacey'. I got him to play me a bit down the phone – remember, this was long before the days of smartphones, so we couldn't just WeTransfer it.

'Bring it on a DAT tape [a kind of digital cassette] –' I said – 'and a cassette version for me, and can you please get here earlier?' Andrew left work early (he actually worked in the tax office) and I set about using the rest of the car journey to write lyrics to a non-existent tune. Feeling panicky didn't cover it, but I came up with something, including a sort of melody that would pretty much fit over anything. As soon as Andrew arrived, I flung the cassette into my Sony Walkman (remember those?) and started rehearsing. I kept it flexible enough to not need to remember it exactly, and it had a long trippy section which I just needed to ad-lib over, so I hoped we get away with it.

Julie found it all quite amusing. 'You're such a worrier,' she said. But as we arrived at the stage door to the venue the very first thing the club manager said was, 'You do have a 20-minute set, don't you?' I swear he smirked; I'm guessing he caught out a few dance acts like that, who came armed only with their A- and B-sides.

Feeling somewhat nervous we took to the stage, did a short version of '7 Ways to Love', followed by 'He is Cola', followed by our trippy new composition, and finished with the 12-inch version of '7 Ways to Love' and – well, we brought the house down. Julie was amazed. 'That track was honestly fantastic,' she said. In our panic, of course we hadn't recorded it, and from that moment it was forgotten. I literally couldn't recall a thing about it the next day; it was as if my unconscious mind allowed me to create it for that urgent moment, and then it was lost. Hey ho, he had to pay us anyways.

We had a hilarious moment getting into a club on one occasion. Often, we would have to try to navigate a huge queue of clubbers trying to get in if there wasn't an accessible back door. One night we arrived at a club in the Midlands late on Saturday night, and there was a huge queue round the block to get in. We pushed our way to the front of the queue, and Julie tried to get the attention of the bouncer. Eventually he heard us, and rising to his full height he said, 'I've not been told anything about a PA tonight.'

'Well, the guys are due on stage in about 10 minutes,' Julie said, and smiled sweetly. He was uninterested – and distracted because there were a couple of extremely attractive, barely dressed girls also trying to check if their name was on the list. Just as we were being jostled, and Julie was trying to get him to allow us in, he let out the loudest fart you've ever heard. He literally stunned himself, and in the fraction of a second it took for him to acknowledge the full prowess of his flatulence (the whole crowd were laughing) we slipped through the barrier, smiling and giving him a thumbs up. He was so pleased with himself! Admission by rip-roaring fart.

We played Greenbelt too. The Greenbelt festival had been part of my life for so many years, and while I'd played a few of the smaller tents, I'd never done main stage, so it was a dream for me. We hired a brilliant performance percussionist, Martin Neil, who I'd worked with in another Christian band, and actually managed a 30-minute set. No idea how!

We tried to capitalise on the whole 'Cola Boy' success. Julie arranged a meeting with Simon Cowell, and she actually got a long way down the line in getting me a deal; they liked the demo tracks we put forward, and they loved the 'Cola Boy' video. It all went downhill when Simon asked Julie my age. Rather foolishly (in hindsight) she told him the truth: 'She's 30.' I'm guessing his lip actually curled. Its seemed that was a bit 'over the hill'.

From that moment I never told anyone my age, and to this day I am incensed by the ageism in the music industry. I have been asked so many times to be interviewed for newspapers and magazines, and they always want your age, even for the tiniest news story about a health product or a new book. I always challenge them and say, 'Not telling you, but if it's a deal-breaker, feel free to make one up. I'm younger than Madonna.' I encouraged journalists to guess, so it was highly amusing that for a few years, I was credited with a range of ages. My friend Haze, of the Circus of Horrors fame, found it hilarious, and would regularly send me letters and cards in the post, addressed to Janey Lee Grace (30). The interesting thing is that when there are articles about men, their age is rarely mentioned.

Over those years I continued to hustle and work with different songwriters. I got a new manager for a while, Harry Cowell, who tried to steer me in a slightly more pop/rock direction. He hooked me up with Rob Davis of Mud fame, and I was a bit star struck, to be honest. At his home studio in Surrey, surrounded by pictures of '80s pop bands, we recorded some tracks together. One, called 'City Never Sleeps', was pretty good, though I say so myself. Harry also connected me with Rockfield Studios. I was already aware of the place because my dear friend Rosi (who later helped with styling for my books) lived near Ross on Wye and had been married to one of the Martinez brothers, who regularly worked with bands there. A couple of years ago, I watched the documentary made about Rockfield Studios, featuring interviews with Queen on the recording of 'Bohemian Rhapsody', Manic Street Preachers, Chris Martin from Coldplay talking about the inspiration for 'Yellow', and of course the sad story of the Charlatans' Rob Collins who died in a car accident near the studios while the band were recording there. It's really well done, definitely worth a watch for music lovers. I stayed there with the main man, Kingsley and his family and worked with a bunch of musicians on some tracks, but sadly everything seemed to fizzle out.

For a while I worked on some songs with the band formed by one of the musicians from Wham!, but that fizzled out too. The truth was, I was a good singer, and not a terrible lyricist, but I couldn't write tunes, and neither could he.

Cola Boy photoshoot

Chapter 17
SOULMATES

Back home, things with Ray were coming to a head, and I started to feel desperate. I recall chatting to Julie on a plane back from Malta where Phil and I had played an outdoor concert. She asked me why I wasn't married to him, and I said, 'Oh God no, I'm a career gal.' She asked if I wanted children, and I laughed out loud and assured her I definitely did not, ever. I remember she said, 'If you're with the right person, you might change your mind about that.'

I knew I wasn't with the right person for me, but what could I do? I was incredibly insecure, co-owned a flat with him and had no idea how I could extricate myself. I didn't want to hurt him. He had a good side, you see, as well as the controlling one. Looking back, I realise he must have been incredibly unhappy too, but I had no idea how I would cope on my own. A lot of women reading this will smile ruefully at that sentence, and that's what keeps people stuck in relationships.

Back to my list of goals: I had been pitching myself to TV stations as a presenter but got no opportunities. Then one day Chris Whatmough rang me and said he had spoken to Sky TV and they needed a new presenter to do their pop music review slot: 'You'll be fantastic babe,' he said. 'Go do the try-out next week.' I remember telling Ray about this incredible exciting opportunity, and his reaction was: 'No, tell them you're not ready, you can't be on TV, look at you, no experience, you'll mess it up.' While I was still reeling from his response, something was about to change forever.

I haven't mentioned my other backing singer mate, Nikki Racklin. She was a talented singer and bass player and lived in a cool flat full of Hendrix posters in Marylebone. We did a few gigs and sessions together, including one supporting Robert Plant at Wembley. One day she rang me and said she had a one-off session and they needed two singers. 'It's an old friend of mine,' she said. 'He is a composer and does music for TV and ads.' I met Nikki at Snake Ranch studios in London and literally felt something odd happening in my stomach as she introduced me to Simon Etchell, who was writing and producing an ad for Coca-Cola. He came into the studio, sat at the piano to teach us the track, and I could feel myself blushing. He had long dark hair, such beautiful blue eyes, and a gorgeous energy. We chatted briefly when we took a coffee break and then when we left, I hounded Nikki and said: 'OMG, he is just gorgeous, how come you didn't warn me!' 'Don't even think about it,' she said. 'He is married. I don't think he is very happy, but he can't seem to leave.' Sounds familiar.

Unbeknown to me, Simon had me been eyeing me up through the studio glass during the session and decided the best way to get to see me again was to hire singers on another session, so he invited Nikki and I back for another gig. This time, Nikki left early and we chatted for longer. He then offered me a lift to GLR where I had to record my show and I got into his huge pink Jaguar, which smelt of dog, and tried not to quiver at being so close to him. A few weeks later, I got another call asking me to do a session for him, with Nikki again (we sure were grateful for the work) but this time in Bromley. I remember that journey in my Mini driving to that godforsaken place for early evening, when studio time was cheaper, and telling Nikki that I could barely drive I was so nervous about seeing him again. Again, Nikki left the session early, and Simon asked if I wanted to grab a coffee.

Just as we were getting ready to leave, my mobile rang (a great brick of a thing) and Chris Whatmough said: 'They want to bring your Sky TV slot forward, they need someone for the day after tomorrow, can you do it? It's just a case of choosing three current artists and their tracks and reviewing them, they'll source the video clips.' I felt so panicky! Ray had made it clear that he didn't think I was ready to be on TV, I had no experience of reviewing pop, and no idea how to choose the best bands, but something in me played the tape forward and I said yes. Simon asked why I was looking so shell-shocked, and I told him all about the offer. I also told him I was fearful, having never done anything like that before, and was unsure what I'd talk about. He beamed with enthusiasm: 'You'll be fantastic,' he said. 'Let's go out now and buy some *Smash Hits* magazines, or whatever, and I'll help you find the right bands to feature, choose artists you know a bit about.'

What a difference! He'd only just met me, yet he believed in me; it made me feel empowered. It also made me realise that I was never going to let Ray hold me back again. It's as if a wall came up around me, and the very next time he told me I shouldn't do something, or criticised my

A fresh faced me in 1982

Barbie and Ken

Luna Park

With Mari Wilson and Julia Fordam

Wham! Working on our dance routines

Wham!'s Club Fantastic Tour – with our hastily cut up tops

George and Andy trying on Pepsi and Shirlie's frocks

Me, George and Andy get the cake

Andy and George. Well earned kip on the tour bus

The Boss

With George during Whamamerica!

Whamamerica! With Brooke Shields in New York

Recording in New York. Me, Dion Estus, Brooke Shields, Andy, Connie Filippello

Wham! Aftershow party with me, George, and trumpet player Paul Spong

On a break in the last Wham! USA Tour

The Wham! girls. Pepsi, Shirlie, Janet and me

The Bee Gees crash our dressing room

More covers gigs

Angie Bowie and me at the Hippodrome

Cola Boy rehearsals for *Top of The Pops*

Summer Roadshow with Nick Heyward

Surfers festival personal appearance for Heartbeat Radio

Traffic crumpet

In concert with Kim Wilde

Publicity shot. I love that dress!

Janey and Simon get married!

Radio 2 calling

The end of an era. Our last pic together

choices, I simply turned away, I didn't engage. It's as if the wall was visible because he seemed to shrink then. In that moment, I took back my power and he never had any hold over me – ever again.

This was augmented by the fact that I was so attracted to Simon. They do talk about love at first sight, and for me it was real. At that point I had no idea if he felt the same way, and I was not going to pursue anything with a happily married man, but just by encouraging me to go and do that TV show (I did, and it was fab, I was Sky News pop reviewer for two years), he showed me that more could be possible for me. That was the point at which I started to become open to the possibility of extricating myself from Ray. It was time.

Simon called me for another couple of sessions across the next few weeks. We joke now about how much that period cost him in session fees, and how utterly unfair it is that I don't get paid for sessions for him now! He was the composer for the BBC TV series *Byker Grove* and his producer started asking why so many of his music clips suddenly included female vocals!

On one occasion we went out for lunch after a recording session for a TV ad and discovered that we were both vegetarian (we aren't now, but that's another story), loved the same kind of music and had a fair bit in common. He was genuinely interested in me, but we didn't touch on our respective relationships; it was enough for me to spend a bit of time in his orbit, I could barely think of anything else. Meanwhile at home I did my utmost to ensure that I was never around at the same time as Ray. I manufactured lots of late gigs with Chris Whatmough, and managed to be working at weekends, communicating by leaving Post-it notes on the fridge. By now we were literally ships passing. It suited me fine.

The turning point came when I decided to go to a Music Industry Conference in Manchester. My best friend from sixth-form college days, Alison, lived there and I thought it would be fun listening to the likes of Feargal Sharkey (who had become a music biz 'suit' by then) and Pete Waterman talking music biz stuff, plus there were always bands playing and great opportunities to meet producers and potentially get gigs. I told Simon I was headed there, and suddenly he had booked his trip too! 'Let's meet in the hotel bar,' he said.

Later that night we walked along by the canal, and he told me he was falling for me, but he was married and didn't want to be the kind of guy that had an affair. I told him I was in a similar situation, though thankfully not married, and we agreed that we'd find a way to get out of our relationships before anything much else happened. We kissed (very romantic down by that canal in Manchester in the rain!) but nothing else. Despite this giving some concern to Nikki, who had brought us together, ('What if it doesn't fit?' she cautioned me) we did not have sex until we had both left our partners for good. Impressive, right?

I told Janet about Simon, and it turned out that her husband, Steve, knew him well from the music biz scene. 'Simon Etchell?' he asked, 'the only muso who sleeps with an AK-47 ready at all times?' Turns out that wasn't strictly the case, though it made a good story among London's session musicians. Simon was, in fact, a target shooter: it was his hobby, and along with another composer friend he had a gun licence and went to a local club in Kent for shooting practice. Of course, a few musos found out about it and thought it highly amusing.

One of Simon's funniest stories was when he was in the running for a gig as MD for Michael Ball on a TV show. He spent the weekend getting ready, even sorting musicians to play in the band. He was prepping a CD of Michael's album given to him by the production company, and as he was listening to one of the tracks with his shooting/composer friend, a call came in from the production company. Michael wanted to use his own MD, and they didn't need him for the gig after all. He didn't know quite how to handle his frustration and said to his mate: 'What shall we do with this now?', holding up the CD with Michael's smiling face on it. 'I'd say target practice,' his mate replied, so they each took a shot at the CD. Bullseye!

Simon became known as the guy who shot Michael Ball.

Years later, when we interviewed Michael on *Steve Wright in the Afternoon*, I told him the story and he found it hilarious. In fact, he asked if Simon had kept the CD so he could have it for his wall. This was, of course, before it became illegal to own handguns, at which point he had to relinquish them all and never did any shooting again.

Chapter 18
RIDING THE AIRWAVES

Once I'd started as a presenter on GLR, I got the radio bug. The truth is, it's addictive; I could never have imagined how much I'd love it. I was doing my gospel show weekly (though it took about two full days to get it together), working four days a week as a traffic reporter for AA Roadwatch (getting up at 4.30 a.m.!) and doing Sky TV every couple of weeks as a music biz reviewer.

While I was at AA Roadwatch, Virgin Radio launched. It was a big deal, and they assigned me to the *Russ and Jono Breakfast Show* as their traffic reporter. They wanted it to be really fun, even though I was delivering important info literally just gleaned from traffic police. We broadcast from the Stanmore studios in North London, and I reported every 20 minutes into the breakfast show. I made it my business to make the traffic report as interesting as possible and spent ages finding different phrases to use: 'The traffic's chocka... it's all agogo now… the Hanger Lane gyratory is doing the twist.' All a bit naff now I think about it, but Russ and Jono loved their 'Traffic crumpet' as they called me (they wouldn't get away with that now!) and it became a bit of a thing as to how much of a chat we'd have live on air after the traffic reports. After a couple of months I got a call from their producer John, who asked me to come into the station — and then offered me my own show on Virgin Radio. It was overnight shows to start – 2 a.m. till 6 a.m., *ouch!* I didn't care, though. I loved it. One of the wishes on the list crossed off: presenter on national radio.

GLR held a leaving party for me in a local pub. I was really touched, even though I'd been very part-time. Those guys had become like family, especially Chris Whatmough, Vanessa Feltz, Danny Baker and, of course, Chris Evans, who also ended up at Virgin not too long after me.

Working at Virgin in the early '90s was a dream. Our studios at Number One Golden Square used to be the home of TV-am, and we had a communal kitchen and green room area where we would hang out, and bands would often do live shows. Some of the most memorable ones were Michael Hutchence, who was unbelievably charismatic. I'd never really been wild about INXS (she ducks!) but suddenly I saw what Paula Yates had seen in him. Elvis Costello played live on one occasion, and I'm mortified to admit even now that I hadn't switched my mobile off, and it rang in a really quiet bit of 'Alison', one of my all-time favourite songs. Seriously – kill me now.

Presenters at Virgin Radio in those early years included the aforementioned Russ Williams and Jono Coleman, plus Tommy Vance (in his leather pants as Jono would say), Graham Dene, Richard Skinner, Emperor Rosko for some shows, Alan 'Fluff' Freeman (the much-loved veteran), Kevin Greening and the only other woman, Wendy Lloyd – till Lynn Parsons joined. Owner Richard Branson would be seen occasionally, and we always got invited to his parties, which were something else. I loved going to parties at the Kensington Roof Gardens, we always had fantastic bands playing at the Virgin parties, and always got VIP treatment at concerts, etc. Richard also invited us all to his 'all Virgin staff' weekends at his country pile. Rocking up to his house in Oxfordshire, the grounds of which had been transformed into an actual fairground, was incredible — and the food was the most fantastic ever.

Record companies loved us, and would give us copious albums, T-shirts and tickets to concerts. I saw so many great gigs: Blur, Oasis, Supertramp… I could have done loads more if I'd had the energy or time. We got to go to album launches, parties and everything in between. Record companies seemed to have a huge amount of money and would ship us all out to a gig somewhere, just for a jolly. We had parties at every unique venue you can think of, from Alton Towers (exclusively for us) through to London Zoo, and I'd never had so much merchandise in my life. Some of my favourite memories were going to see Crowded House at the relatively small Bush Hall in Shepherds Bush, and Chris Rea at the same venue for an album launch.

While the social life at Virgin rocked, I didn't much love the politics. In the seven years I was a presenter there, we had no less than six programme controllers. Each would swan in, try to ring the changes, fire a few people – 'new broom, clean sweep', and all that – and generally cause a bit more chaos before disappearing with their tail between their legs.

A few of them I genuinely can't even recall, but I do remember with some fondness an American woman called Suzy. She was nice enough but we wondered about her 'grasp' of British radio. Most of the Virgin DJs had come from Radio 1, Radio Luxembourg or similar, all stars in their own right. When she held her compulsory presenters' meetings once a week, she would try to stress that for a commercial station like Virgin, our own personality simply didn't matter. 'You're marketing men,' she would declare, and the likes of Richard Skinner, Tommy Vance and Graham Dene would shuffle uncomfortably in their seats, not wishing to sound egotistical but knowing full well that the UK audience cared far more about engaging with the presenters than hearing another advert for a mobile phone, the latest sanitary product or the ad for Bacardi Blue (a fantastic ad if I remember rightly!)

We worked to a tight format, for sure: there was no straying from the playlist, and Virgin prided themselves on having a relatively small library of tracks. 'It's all been tested with focus groups,' they'd tell us. 'Listeners tend to stay with us for a maximum of 15 minutes, on a short drive, or getting ready for work, etc. In those minutes they want to hear tracks they love, so we need to constantly play the tried-and-tested hits.' (Um … perhaps listeners stayed only 15 minutes because we played the same tracks all the time!) Sadly, it turned me – and those of us who LOVED pop music – into jaded cynics. I got to the point where I felt as if I had to play Del Amitri one more time I'd go insane. To this day, that repetition has spoiled whole genres of music for me.

'Classic Album tracks and the best new music' was the Virgin Radio strapline, and we had to trip that off the tongue regularly. Jono once spent hours scratching off the letters 'AL' off all the posters and even defacing the mugs in the building, so that when some important dignitaries came in, everything they saw said: 'Classic ...Bum Tracks'.

The management lived and died by RAJAR (a system that measures audience numbers) constantly knee-jerking as to how they could get the figures up, to bring in more ad revenue. They regularly brought in consultants – who were, I'm guessing, paid a small fortune and, just like Suzy, had little understanding of British radio listeners. One guy came from Australia and tried to make his mark. Behind his back we were disparaging, I can tell you, but we went along with his ideas. He decided that we must work as a team, and that everyone from the highest management suit down to the security guard and the cleaner should form part of a consultation about what was working and what wasn't in their experience of being a Virgin radio employee. He called it The Big Jump and it cost a fortune, including lots of questionnaires, and one-to-one interviews with every single person on the payroll. Jono, true to form, christened it The Big Dump and changed as much of the paperwork as he could get his hands on. Of course, rumours circulated as to what was said in those confidential interviews, some of it published when the project finally ended. The conclusion seemed to be that the majority of people were unhappy with various aspects of… the management! But, of course, rather than firing anyone from the upper floors, a couple of DJs got their marching orders and everyone had to try to pretend it would all go swimmingly well from then on in. Robin Banks was one of the casualties then; he was a sweet guy but always a mix of edgy and comical. He once cost the station a small fortune for making a gag about a notorious, but still open, criminal case. The station got fined and never stopped complaining about it despite his apology.

Chapter 19
BURNING THE CANDLE AT BOTH ENDS

On overnights at that point, I would arrive at the station around 1 a.m., do the show from 2 to 6, then drive back to Hertfordshire to sleep for a few hours. That was six nights a week, then my *Sunday Brunch* show was on ITV (more on that later) and I had to drive up to Nottingham on Saturday to rehearse and meet the guests.

Even though I didn't get home till 7.15 a.m. every day, Virgin programme directors would make the presenters meeting, usually held at midday on Thursdays, compulsory for all presenters. I still can't believe I swallowed that, sleeping for literally two hours before needing to get up and get a train back into the station, to listen to a bit of bickering about advertisements and promotional campaigns before getting the train home again for a few more hours before that night's show. When Jonathan Ross was at the station, it was joyous to see that he just didn't care. One morning (his show followed mine on a Saturday for a while) he slated the management live on air. 'There's this new guy,' he said scornfully, 'he's a bit of a tosser, hasn't got a clue'.

When we got to programme controller Number 4, I got worried. I'd managed to keep my head down with the US and Australian controllers, but the latest was a guy called Sean, who knew British radio well. We knew as soon as we met him that like many new managers, wanting to 'make their mark', he could be out for blood. None of us knew who he might oust. I had an inkling it might be me but wasn't sure what I might do to upset him. I didn't have to wait very long to find out. On his second night on the job, he called me live on air around 3 a.m. and said, 'I'm listening'. *Hmm, no pressure there*, but irrespective of me sounding OK, the technology in those days was such that the carts (which held the advertisements) were very temperamental. We were trialling a new system that always seemed to go wrong in the middle of the night, when there were no technical staff around – well, no staff at all – just me and the security guard.

It was a fairly regular occurrence for an ad not to play, or the traffic news not to come in on time, and in commercial radio nothing is more important than doing the presenter reads that you're given, playing in the ads, in the exact order they are scheduled, presenting the station idents and hitting the news on time. For a station like Virgin, that could be a tricky little sequence because we had to fire ads, read station idents and ensure correct timings – and if an ad didn't play in, or the traffic reporter vanished from the other end of the line, we had to fill, so that it would still sound seamless.

The night of Sean listening in was a disaster: a whole ad block didn't play in correctly, so I had to delay it and call in the tech support. Poor Fiona, our tech guru, was constantly being woken in the night and having to taxi in to work. She blamed me for her relationship ending.

I knew how important those ads were, it was the only reason we had a job – 'marketing men', remember. I was extremely good at keeping to time, but sometimes the tech had other ideas. I spoke to Sean the following day and Fiona happened to be nearby to back up my report of the ads failing, but with unsmiling eyes he said: 'Make sure it doesn't happen again.'

The following night was better, the ads played in, and it was a good show, until the last segment into the 5 a.m. news. The format was that we had to play an ad, then say the holy words: 'This is Virgin' (or something like that) and then hit the jingle to lead into the news. We had about 20 seconds leeway, max. On this occasion I fired the ad, but it didn't play. I waited a couple of seconds (forever in radio time) but it wasn't cueing up, so I 'vamped', repeated a strapline, said: 'This is Virgin', hit the jingle a few seconds early, said: 'This is Virgin' again, then into the news. Straight after the news I did another ident, then played the ads, which had by then decided to cue up.

I'd been in bed about one hour when the phone rang. I staggered out of bed, wondering who had died, to find it was Sean, calling me at 7.45 a.m., when he knew I'd finished my shift at 6 a.m., to say he was 'very disappointed' that I hadn't closely followed the station ident guidelines. I explained exactly what had happened with the ad not firing, my split-second decision to go to news a few seconds early, and I apologised for saying the ID line twice in my slight panic. He said he would see me in his office for a meeting the next day. I knew that was it. He needed to fire someone, and I was such an easy target. Who cares about the overnight gal?

In tears, I rang Chris Whatmough, who by then was working at Radio 2. 'FFS darling,' he said, 'I know Sean from long ago, I'll have a word. Don't worry, I won't say you told me.'

Oh, how I wish I could have been a fly on the wall at that meeting! Apparently, Chris called Sean, and took him out for a drink. They chatted about radio generally, and Chris said: 'You've got some girl on overnights, haven't you? She's really good, I'd be thinking she's the one to watch.'

Sean never did bother me again, we got along just fine after that! Thank you, Chris, God rest your soul!

One of the finest moments from Virgin Radio, which I have dined out on over the years, is the saga of the notorious weekly feature 'No Repeat Thursday'. An interesting idea that may not have been deemed at all appropriate on a radio station where the music was incredibly varied. On Radio 2, we didn't expect the same artist to be played during the day (apart from perhaps a playlist current chart hit) let alone the same track, but because Virgin was so repetitive I suppose it was a challenge to play completely different tracks all day. So, in a bid to get keen listeners listening for longer, they offered a prize, something like £2000 to the first caller to phone in upon hearing a repeated track. Of course, keen listeners would eagerly ring up and say: 'I heard Blondie twice! "Atomic!"' 'Sorry, no deal. It was "Heart of Glass". Thanks for calling!'

Of course, we suspected that the idea was that a track would never be repeated, but we only knew about our own show. Management instilled in us all to follow our playlist sheets religiously and be extra-careful not to put on the wrong album track. We all HATED Thursdays: it was so stressful, the playlist sheets had faint print, and I was terrified of making an error and being the one to cost the station money. At one meeting, programme director Suzy told us that if we made that mistake, the prize money might come off our wages. I remember Trevor White, who was to us Virgin presenters what Tommy Eyre was to Wham!'s backing band, telling her in no uncertain terms that would not be happening, that presenters were not going to be in jeopardy of failing their mortgage payments because some marketing director hadn't sewn up his crazy promo idea (or something like that). Trevor had our back.

Not long after that conversation, having been promoted to the 10 p.m. to 2 a.m. shift, I took over from a DJ I'll call Jake. A fantastic DJ but a man of few words off the air. Ever the professional but not the easiest to get to know. He had quite an acerbic wit and just did his thing, then left, rarely getting involved in any of the station shenanigans. I arrived one Thursday night to hear phones ringing in the offices. Once upstairs I popped into the green room to an array of phone lights flashing. Often, when waiting for my show, I'd answer them: it was quite fun to talk to callers and get a few dedications, but first, I decided to pop into the studio to get my all-important running order. There was only one studio – hot seating, we called it. I opened the door to the studio and Jake was rigid, and pale as a sheet. He stared at me and said in a clipped voice, 'Don't… answer… the… phone...'

'What phone?' I said, and he told me, in a weak desperate voice, that he had just realised that he had played a repeat track on 'No Repeat Thursday.' But not just one track… a WHOLE hour's worth of tracks that had been played earlier in the day. I mean, come on, it's an easy mistake to make, you simply pick up the wrong track sheet. I couldn't get out of the studio fast enough to crack up laughing, and I suddenly knew why every phone light was flashing. The doorbell started to ring continuously, we had to ask the security guy to keep it locked, and I couldn't do any of my regular features which involved inviting callers.

I'm not completely certain how it was all resolved, but I can only assume Jake had to face the (repetitive) music and call the management. There would be literally no way a 'first' caller could have been ascertained, so I think they ended up coughing up cash to a few lucky punters and I think the feature quietly disappeared for a while, – but it remains one of the funniest moments in the back room of radio history.

* * *

Throughout this time, in addition to being full-time at Virgin, I still presented my weekly Sky TV slot – and I've no idea how I found time, but I was also presenting on an ad hoc basis on VH1. I was based in the same studios as MTV and was a bit like their older sister, featuring contemporary rock and more alternative artists. I was asked to host a live, all-day rock event, and it was unbelievably chaotic. I did it, though; live radio had given me such great experience. I met Davina McCall while I was at VH1; she was on MTV but helping out on the live event, and we were both in the make-up room.

The make-up artists often worked on several of us at the same time, so at one point I was sitting there with my hair in rollers and face shiny and squeaky clean before any make-up was applied (never the best look). Craig Charles (famous for *Red Dwarf* at that point) came in, was introduced, quickly got his make-up done, and left. About 40 minutes later, he popped back into the make-up room, and by then my hair had been blow-dried (proper '80s big hair) and I had full make-up on. 'Christ!' he exclaimed, doing a double take. 'The Blonde cleans up alright!'

I think that was a compliment.

I loved doing TV, but I had no agent or contacts to get onto a mainstream show. That was about to change when I went to a music biz party with Chris and met a guy who was a TV producer. 'I'm about to produce a new Sunday morning show for ITV,' he said. 'We're looking for a presenter, we think it will probably be Jan Leeming.' 'Can I audition?' I asked, and I think he was so taken aback by my forwardness he gave me his card. A few days later, reading from an autocue and interviewing one of their producers mimicking a live guest, I delivered my finest. It came naturally to me because I'd been doing radio for ages.

He told me he would get back to me, and later called and said that his bosses had thought Jan might be a 'safe pair of hands', being older and experienced and all that, but he wanted to find someone relatable and friendly. He had shown the audition tapes to his daughter and she had immediately picked me out. They hired me. I never did get to thank her! True to form, Ray was adamant that I shouldn't accept the job – the 'you're not ready' thing again – but I think he knew that I wasn't listening anymore. Simon, of course, was as delighted as me that I'd got the gig.

It shows how green I was: Nigel had his secretary Lynn call me to discuss the fee for the TV show which was appallingly low, and I just said…OK. 'Are you sure you don't want to negotiate?' she said, and I realised that it was then I should have laughed and said: 'Add a few noughts.' Bless Lynn, she realised I hadn't done this before, and managed to find a bit more money in the pot for me under the guise of extra production fees – just as well, as I lined up a fair few of the guests.

Sunday Brunch was ITV's Sunday morning 'religious' magazine programme, and my co-presenter was Julian

Going for the Bardot look

Pettifer. I was terrified that he wouldn't like them bringing in a newbie, but he was just charming. I learned fast. Fortunately Julian handled the serious news or political stories, and I did the more touchy-feely stuff and the on-location interviews, including one with Linus Roach for the film *Priest*. Live TV was incredibly stressful, but fortunately being used to live radio and my Sky News slots, I found it came relatively easily. I remember one harrowing moment, though, when a guest froze on me. The show came from Nottingham at 11 a.m. on Sunday morning. I would typically drive up the night before, and we'd rehearse and then have dinner with any guests scheduled for the show, in order to get to know them and 'warm them up'. I recall chatting to a vicar, who had been hired to do an interview with me on the power of prayer. We discussed it over dinner, in a conversational way. He seemed fine, obviously knew his stuff, but the next day, as he sat opposite me in the studio, the cameras rolled, and I could see from the look on his face that he was not going to be able to utter one word. He was literally like a rabbit caught in the headlights. The producers whispered in my earpiece, 'Vamp till he calms down.' FFS, this was live TV! I think I rambled on to camera about how prayer is so often used in a crisis, while silently sending calming vibes to him. He managed to compose himself, just about, and we got a couple of answers

In Jerusalem with Julian and *Sunday Brunch*

in. That experience formed the basis of the media training I do now. Rocking up to an interview thinking you know your stuff won't cut it: you need your key angles, your key message instilled in you and rehearsed, and you need the muscle memory along with the knowledge, so that even if you freeze, you'll be able to access the key points you wanted to make.

Mostly though, *Sunday Brunch* ran smoothly. We had a well-received segment with Tony Robinson, and always had an entertainment slot. On one occasion they shipped me off to interview Sam Fox, she of Page Three fame, who had found God apparently.

I had to quickly learn to smarten up for TV. I couldn't wear my usual rock 'n' roll attire, so Simon took me shopping and helped me find some clothes that were a bit more suitable for daytime television. I remember fondly a fabulous red top with long sleeves and a heart emblazoned on the front, and a mustard-coloured suede suit with a waistcoat and mini skirt, which I wore with opaque black tights. ITV received a letter of complaint about my skirt, saying it was not respectful on a religious programme to be wearing a short skirt. Honestly, people had time on their hands!

Despite some viewers finding it risqué, the critics clearly thought it way too tame. Victor Lewis-Smith, renowned for his wit and bile, wrote a scathing review. After slating the format of the show and the segment with Tony Robinson and the 'pathetic' gormless guests on the episode he had seen, he turned his attention to the presenters: 'Julian Pettifer and Janey Lee Grace are so anodyne they look as though they have been knitted. Janey Lee Grace is so pure she makes Mother Teresa look like a whore!'

That's going on the gravestone!

Chapter 20
AN ULTIMATUM

Simon and I had been meeting up frequently, and it became clear that we were more than attracted to each other. His situation was, on the one hand, simple. He had been married for seven years to someone he didn't love, and yes, when he told me that, my first thought was also *I'm not buying into the 'Be my mistress...my wife doesn't understand me' BS*, but he really did seem genuine when he shared that he'd 'fallen into' marriage. They had no children, and did very little together. He was (and still is), extremely kind, however, and at the time was literally terrified of hurting her.

I understood that, of course. Time had definitely run out on my own relationship, but I just didn't know how to get out. The answer came from my dear singing buddy, Janet. One day she said: 'Leave him, just come and live with us for a while, we will do a mate's rate on the rent.' So that was that. I continued to pay the mortgage on the flat, left most of my stuff there but moved in with Janet, her husband and new baby. Fortunately, the house was big enough for me to sleep at the top after a night shift at Virgin Radio and not be disturbed by either the baby crying, Janet doing opera scales, or her husband (who had been a brass player for Wham!) practising. It suited us. I was beyond grateful for that act of kindness, and asked her once why she did it for me, when I didn't know how I could really pay her back. She said, wisely, 'It's karma, isn't it, it will come back to me in other ways.'

Despite the fact that I had all but left Ray, and was renting a room at Janet's, Simon was still in his marital home. He kept telling me he would leave, but it didn't seem to be happening quickly. I most definitely did not want to be 'the mistress' and so I suggested that we needed to stop meeting up for a time, so that he could decide what he wanted. It was hard to make that call, though. He regularly met me before my Virgin show for a drink and we spent hours on the phone every day. Sometimes he came up to see me at Virgin or the TV studios. I remember one scary night when I nearly had Ray and Simon in the Virgin Radio reception at the same time. But as I've already said, there was nothing going down: I was determined to get out free from baggage and forever, or not get out at all. A girlfriend suggested that Simon was perhaps a procrastinator, or fearful of change, and that I should give him an ultimatum. I got that opportunity when I went away for three weeks and let him know that if nothing had changed when I got back, I'd have no contact with him for a year. Sounds very dramatic, but I meant it.

That opportunity came courtesy of *Sunday Brunch*. The producer wanted to host our Easter Sunday show from Jerusalem and leave no stone unturned in the reporting. I'd never been to Israel before. Of course I was excited to go, and after much arguing with the managers at Virgin, I got three weeks off and experienced a life-changing trip.

My main companion was TV producer, Bruce, who knew Jerusalem well, so I got to go to the best cafés and restaurants and loved it. We were staying in a Christian Palestinian run hotel right in the old city, with a beautiful courtyard garden featuring a fountain, where I'd have coffee before the day started.

We interviewed Palestinians and Jews alike, asking how they could practise their faith and coexist peacefully. It seems way too simplistic now, doesn't it?, but honestly, our programme was exploring how they integrated. That's not to say I didn't get a shock to see the reality of life there. I couldn't get my head around the sheer number of young soldiers on the streets, and one night when I was fast asleep in my hotel room, I woke suddenly and froze in terror because there was a soldier stepping in through my balcony door, gun in hand.

'Are you OK, ma'am?' he asked. I nodded, too terrified to speak, and he said he was checking because I'd left my balcony door open. It was hot.

We travelled to the West Bank, did the usual tourist stuff in Bethlehem, and had a very moving experience of recording some interviews at the House of Hope, an orphanage in Jerusalem. Good Friday was a monumental day. A tour guide accompanied us and we followed the Stations of the Cross. I recorded it all on audio too and interviewed with the guide. It was very moving, and along the route we saw impromptu performances – by pop-up drama companies, I suppose. One involved an incredibly poignant portrayal of Jesus, naked but for a loin cloth and dragging a huge cross along the rough terrain while passers-by (pre-assigned, I assume) threw blood at him (tomato sauce does look realistic). We had to move on, so I couldn't stay to see how they portrayed the Crucifixion.

On a happier note, I also got to paddle on the shore of Lake Galilee and soak up the April sunshine, but there I had a moment of utter sadness.

In a few days the trip would end, and I'd heard nothing from Simon. I guessed that he just hadn't been able to leave after all and was probably thinking I'd see him anyway. I wouldn't. I knew that was it, but I felt as though my heart had been ripped out. 'Cheer up,' Bruce said, as he bundled us back into the minibus back from Galilee. 'Plenty more fish in the Dead Sea, I will make you fishers of men,' he quipped, singing a Sunday school chorus – but I was far from OK.

That night, back in my hotel room and with the balcony door firmly locked, the phone rang. 'Do you prefer Richmond or Primrose Hill? I've seen two flats and it's hard to choose.' He had actually done it, found a flat, and he moved out as I was returning from Israel.

Back in the UK, I moved out of Janet's flat and in with Simon. We loved living in Primrose Hill, bumping into Bobby Gillespie at the shops and finding our second home in the vegetarian restaurant Manna, but it was hideously expensive especially because Simon was still paying for his marital home in Kent and I was still paying half the mortgage on my flat. We were both concerned about our exes, but determined we were going to stay together.

Sometime later, Simon filed for divorce and I properly left Ray, SO grateful we had never got married. I practically gave the flat to him (I just wanted to be kind, but wow, I lost a lot on that deal). And Simon's divorce, which should have been simple – seven years, no children – became one of the most complex in history.

Chapter 21
COOL OR CHEESY?

Despite being a full-on pop and rock presenter, across the years, I hadn't completely eschewed wearing my gospel music hat. I connected with Michael Wakelin, a radio and TV producer working on religious docs and *Songs of Praise*, and in addition to getting me featured on *Songs of Praise* with one of my tracks, he encouraged me to come up with a pitch for a documentary for Radio 1. We wanted to introduce the idea that Contemporary Christian music was not naff, which was no mean feat because most of the stuff around was a bit crap. Most people only knew of happy-clappy music, and apart from Sixpence None the Richer, who did more for Contemporary Christian music than any other band, there wasn't much decent God-fearing music. Michael came up with the title 'Jesus – Cool or Cheesy?', which I told him in no uncertain terms was terrible. Radio 1 bought it – rumour has it, on the title alone!

Of course, we had to bring in the US connections as there really were no UK bands to speak of, so we headed off on a whirlwind trip to the states to get the lowdown on the Contemporary Christian music scene. Simon got an air ticket and tagged along for the first leg of our trip, which was Nashville. For a muso not to have visited Nashville was actually a travesty, so we had to put that right. Before Michael landed in Nashville, we did the rounds of the music biz haunts, enjoying the fact that there was a gitvox (a guitarist who also sang) in a cowboy hat on the junction of every single highway. They clearly wouldn't be getting any cash from busking, but maybe if the traffic backed up, and a window was wound down, they'd be spotted and catapulted to stardom…who knows?

Simon and I hired a car and headed to Graceland. I hadn't put myself down as an especially big Elvis Fan, but it wasn't long after the release of Mark Cohn's 'Walking in Memphis', so of course I was excited to see the tourist sites. And I was blindsided by the emotion I felt at Graceland. I loved every bit of that touristy trip, from soaking up the atmosphere in the Elvis Jungle Room, standing by the grave with 'An American Trilogy' playing and touring Sun Studio, to staying in a typically naff motel with a guitar-shaped pool (obvs), being asked if: 'Ya'll want grits?' in the diner and literally 'walking with my feet ten feet off of Beale.'

Back in Nashville we joined in with some line dancing (hilarious, and SO much harder than you think) and Simon and I had to produce our passports before we were allowed to buy a drink at a bar. 'I'm guessing you guys must be vegetarian?' the bartender said with a Texan drawl. Apparently, we looked under 21 despite being about 35!

From there, Michael and I flew to LA. I'd been before with Wham! and knew what to expect, but it really was a working trip, so we literally saw only the inside of the hotel, the hire car and the studios where we interviewed various producers and artists. If I recall correctly, we spoke to Leanne Rimes' producer, interviewed the leading Christian rap artists of the day, DC Talk, and even got an audience with Sixpence None the Richer ('Kiss Me' was still riding high in the charts). Back in Primrose Hill, Simon and I edited the documentary and it ran on Radio 1 with a great review in the *Sunday Times* by leading critic Gillian Reynolds. I still think the title was terrible, though.

I made another couple of documentaries for Radio 1 and spent a lot of time bugging Michael to get me a gig on *Songs of Praise* or similar. He never did manage that, but sometime later, when I had joined Radio 2, they did run a feature on me when I had a couple of tracks out as an album. I'd recorded a version of the hymn 'Be Thou My Vision', and they filmed me striding into BBC Radio 2 and doing the factoids. To this day I am amazed Steve Wright agreed to that: he was very private, and didn't like being on camera much. I think he really said yes because he knew it meant a lot to me. Then the film cut to me singing the track as I wandered over some Cotswold Hills. It was absolutely freezing, windy and spitting with rain, and my hair was splattered across my face. I could see the look they were going for – windswept on the hills – but it's hard even to lip-sync when your hair is in your mouth. When it was broadcast on *Songs of Praise*, Simon's auntie Iris said she had proudly watched it with her friend June, who said: 'She's miming!' To which Iris replied, 'Certainly not! Janey's a proper singer!'

I was amazed how many people told me they'd seen that *Songs of Praise* feature. When I asked if they usually watched the show they said, 'Course not!' Seems as though everyone was at their aunts that Sunday.

Chapter 22
TEA BAGS

Simon and I stayed in the flat in Primrose Hill for nigh on a year, but it was frighteningly expensive. We toyed with the idea of renting somewhere out of town but we were still entangled in finances with exes, so there was no urgency. One Saturday we decided to go out for a drive and ended up in Hertfordshire. After cappuccinos at a garden centre, we had a pub lunch and then realised we needed tea bags, so dropped down off the A1 into Brookmans Park. It's a kooky little village with some posh houses and a few shops. I'd vaguely heard of it as being the childhood home of Tracey, from Everything but the Girl (which she would later describe in detail, in her fantastic book *Another Planet*). As we walked across the green, we talked about houses, agreeing that we both loved high ceilings. At the shops, we looked in the window of an estate agent. There was a small church for sale, already converted. 'Let's go see it, just for fun,' Simon said, and the agent drove us straight there. Turns out it was, too small, dark and not the right energy. 'There is another place,' the agent said, 'literally just come on the market, I haven't typed the details yet, but you might like it, it's unique, huge double high hallway – you mentioned a high ceiling.' 'Why not?' we said, feeling a bit like those annoying people we've all read about who spend their weekends nosing around properties they have no intention of buying.

We rocked up outside a huge house that had originally been a big bungalow but had been converted to have a massive, 40-foot lounge a grand circular staircase, and the highest ceiling ever! It was totally pop star, with a beautiful garden and a big outdoor swimming pool. We chatted with the owner, who was selling because her husband had died and there were too many memories. 'It's beautiful,' we said, 'huge spaces.' 'How might you use the space?' she asked, and Simon said: 'I'd have a grand piano over there,' gesturing to one of the kooky corners of the huge lounge. She looked a bit teary-eyed, and said her husband was musical and would have loved that too.

We made an offer that was ridiculously low, but it was all we knew we could get with the financial mess we were both in, and I think because she liked us, she accepted it. The next adventure began. We had literally gone out for tea bags and bought a house! Simon had a personal bank manager at Nat West at the time (imagine that now!) and he pulled it out the bag, set up a joint mortgage and got the ball rolling. We agreed not to tell our respective exes till we knew for sure, but the bank had other ideas. They addressed the mortgage docs to the flat I had lived in with Ray, and to the home of Simon's wife. The envelopes were addressed to Simon Etchell and Janey Lee Grace, with 'Important Mortgage Documents enclosed'. *Ouch!*

We made it happen, and in as compassionate a way as possible, mostly by being ultra-generous with our exes. We moved into our Brookmans Park home with just a few personal belongings, and often joke about the fact that we literally owned only a butter dish!

It was a fabulous home for a few years: the pool parties became infamous, and we even hosted a fantastic art gallery day there, as we loved 'outsider art' and wanted to showcase an artist we'd met in Cornwall. Those were extravagant years: we had decent incomes, Simon was writing music for TV, film and adverts; I had my Virgin Radio gig and some TV work; and we had no children. We weren't planning any. It was never really discussed, but life felt too complex with our respective exes who were both finding it hard to move on. Simon's divorce, which really should have been a simple rubber-stamping, became unbelievably complex. Our lawyer became so intrinsically involved that he became a friend, but that didn't stop him putting the clock on at £250 an hour, even for the time it took for Simon to give him a lift into London for a pre-court hearing! This went on for years.

Me and Simon moving in day at Brookmans Park

With Simon in Brookmans Park

Talking of exes, when we had been living at the Brookmans Park house for a few years, I had a call from my first love, Mark. He had kept in touch a bit over the years, sharing news of his life in Brazil with his wife and four children. He said he was going to be in the UK, so I invited him over. Mark arrived and once he realised that Simon was a musician and composer, he made a beeline for Simon's studio. They spent ages in there, with Mark remembering his talents on the guitar, then Simon stayed home while Mark and I popped out. I wanted to take him somewhere nice, as he hadn't been in the UK much, so we drove to Sopwell House in St Albans, to their fancy bar where you could have afternoon tea and cocktails. As we caught up on old times, we noticed that alongside us on the nice squishy couches were David and Victoria Beckham. I couldn't have wished for a better coincidence!

Mark left having had a nice time, I hoped. It was lovely to see him. I can't help but wonder though, if a part of him wished he'd found me squatting in a shared flat on the bones of my arse trying to make a living as a singer, rather than happily living the dream with a gorgeous guy who was a wealthy composer in a fabulous home, loving my role as a presenter on Virgin Radio, having had a pretty successful singing career.

Christmas 1997 was memorable. Simon and I stayed with one of my oldest friends, Rosi, at her cottage near Monmouth. The weather was absolutely terrible, storms and ferocious winds, but holed up in her cottage, with supplies for Christmas Day, we were super cosy – till there was a power cut. We found it highly amusing as we walked down the hill in the dark to go to midnight Mass at the church, thankfully a candlelit event, but we weren't quite so amused when Christmas Day rolled around and there was still no power whatsoever. Fortunately, Rosi had an open fire, so we put potatoes and veggies in the fire, and found a camping stove to cook some other bits on. I felt a bit ill, though, and was very clumsy knocking over a whole bottle of champagne. Rosi was not pleased!

A couple of weeks after that, I had some worrying symptoms around my menstrual cycle. I was bleeding between periods and having some dizzy spells. The doctor thought I had an ovarian cyst. I was shocked, having never been ill really, and determined never to be. She offered to send a referral letter for a scan, which she said would come through in roughly three weeks, but I said, *No, I'll pay privately and do it straight away*. I was very upset, not knowing if it would mean I'd need an operation, so asked Simon to come with me to the private hospital. In the radiographer's room, I was praying silently: *Please let this be small, please let me not need an operation.*

The radiographer moved the ultrasound scan around and pointed to the screen. Here are some small fibroids, she said. I was impatient: *Yes, yes and what about the cyst*! 'And this –' she interrupted me – 'is your baby.'

What???

Chapter 23
AND THEN THERE WERE THREE

It's a good thing I was lying down. It seems I had a seven-week foetus, and Simon couldn't be more delighted. Suddenly I went from not wanting a baby to wanting this one desperately. But all wasn't plain sailing because I'd been bleeding. 'It can happen,' she said, 'you've every chance of it being OK.' The consultant thought differently. 'It's 50/50,' he said. 'Keep your legs and fingers crossed, and rest.' I went home in shock, dazed and stunned, and terrified, but I went on a steep learning curve, and decided that if there was a 50 per cent chance of keeping it, I'd focus on that.

I took a few days off work, and Simon bought me a huge stack of books on natural pregnancy and birth. I was so green, I knew nothing, other than I wouldn't be doing anything conventionally. It was around that time that I read an article about Harry Enfield's wife, Lucy. The title was something like: 'It took 17 people for this baby's safe arrival.' The article talked about Lucy's reflexologist, masseur, reiki practitioner and a whole host of other supporters. Plus, it said, she chose to have the baby at the Hospital of St John & St Elizabeth in St John's Wood in London, where water births were the norm. I rang them the next day and booked in for another ultrasound scan. Simon came with me again, and we were shown into one of the lovely birthing rooms. The staff were just lovely, totally holistic. I felt in safe hands. I knew in that moment that I couldn't give birth anywhere else.

Discovering I was pregnant and knowing I wanted to do it as naturally as possible, suddenly threw everything into focus for me. It took me right back to when I had first become interested in the whole concept of Mind Body Spirit.

Years ago, at Ray's parent's home, I had found an old dog-eared first edition book from the early '50s on natural cures. Until then I'd never heard of naturopathy, heliotherapy or apitherapy (the healing power of honey) or delved into the world of spirituality and mindset. It led me down all kinds of rabbit holes, and I started to recognise the importance of focusing on what we want, visualising and goal setting. The next day, after reading it in one sitting, I decided to write a wish list of what I wanted:

> *I will present a mainstream radio show (I obviously meant Radio 1)*
>
> *I will be a main or support act on a UK tour*
>
> *I will be a music biz presenter on TV*

– and some rather obvious personal stuff, along the lines of

> *I am in a fulfilling and loving relationship* (I meant a new one!)

I stopped short of saying: *And I will have babies…*

All the items on that wish list came true, though not in exactly the way I had envisaged, but the universe certainly seemed to have surprises in store for me. They do say, *be careful what you wish for, it just might come true!*

I told the gang at Virgin when I was three months pregnant, and of course a few of them said they'd already guessed, but I was well, thankfully, blooming really. I'm very grateful that I had no morning sickness or problems. My due date was 28 August 1998.

Sonny, true to nature, came right on time, and despite me wanting a water birth, he had different ideas, and landed firmly on the ground after a bonkers long labour. If I'd been in a regular hospital, I'd definitely have been induced, but because this was John and Lizzies (as it was affectionately known) I was simply kept comfortable while reflexologists worked on certain pressure points, and midwives did reiki and massaged my back.

By Day Two we strolled out into the sunshine in St John's Wood, and all was well. Day Four saw us taking Sonny to the Greenbelt music festival for the day. I didn't want to miss it, and so we wrapped him up and made sure his ears were protected and didn't stand too near the speakers. He was without doubt the youngest festivalgoer in that field in Northampton, rocking to 'Brimful of Asha' because Cornershop were headlining.

I didn't realise how popular Virgin Radio was, but a week or so after Sonny's birth I was offered an 'at home photo shoot' with *OK!* magazine. Of course, we said OK, but looking back I wished we'd asked for a bit more money! It was a hell of a day, constantly being made up till we were orange, and hours of waiting around to get the right shots. Sonny was incredibly well behaved, bless him, but finally

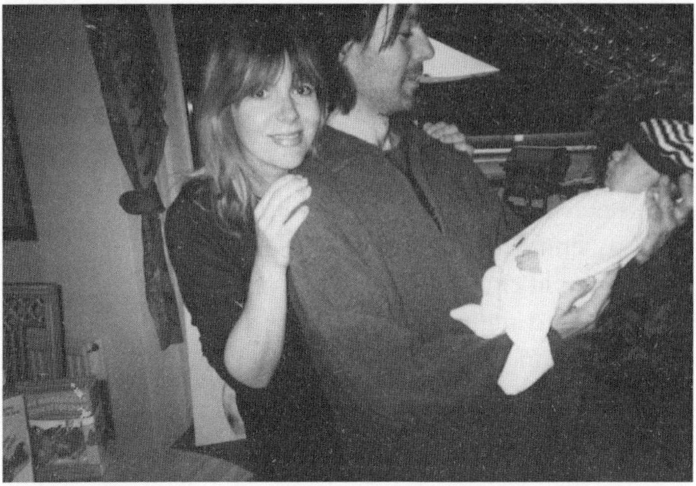

And then we were three – Me, Simon and Sonny

he decided to cry and wouldn't stop. Some of the pics are of me cradling him trying to pretend he wasn't bellowing!

We had a five-page spread in *OK!* magazine. I'm unsure it was good for anything other than ego, but we laugh at it now. Simon's ex took it as a reason to call the lawyers, , perhaps suspecting that we had been paid a fortune. I wish! The lawyer's fees responding to it all probably cost far more.

Of course, during the first pregnancy, I had worried that having a baby might impair my career. Lily Allen made a big splash recently, saying having children had ruined hers. I'd never planned to have children, so I figured it might change my ambition and make it harder for me to get work. The opposite was true. Having a baby gave me so much confidence and identity; I felt that if I could achieve that, I could do anything.

As we had no family nearby, getting childcare wasn't simple. Simon worked from his home studio so he could look after Sonny when I was at work, but with breastfeeding there is only so much milk that can be expressed. I went back to work after only a couple of months, and Simon would drive in to collect me, bringing Sonny with him. Then I'd breastfeed him (sometimes on air; it was just as well there was no one else in the building!) and then he'd drive us home. I was grateful for that late-night show, it meant I could pop on 'Stairway to Heaven', feed Sonny and then Simon could whip him back into the green room as I opened the mic for the next link. Soon after that I started doing early breakfast at the weekends, while we were still in the same regime, and Jonathan Ross's show would follow mine. He would sometimes be in early and thought it was hilarious that I was feeding Sonny while on air. There was many a Saturday morning when Jonathan walked around prepping for his show and holding my baby. Seems surreal now. Sonny, now 25, is quite impressed.

Chapter 24
RADIO 2 CALLING!

One day I got a call from Michael Wakelin. He told me that the production team in Manchester had the opportunity to pitch for an early morning slot on BBC Radio 2 on Saturdays, a sort of showcase for new talent. 'Record a demo,' he said. 'You never know, we could produce the show.' I was convinced that they wouldn't be interested in me, and really had no time to do a demo, but I felt bad letting Michael down, so one night after my Virgin shift, I moved into the tiny news cubicle, grabbed a few Radio 2ish records and did a very off-the-cuff demo. I popped the CD in the post to Michael and forgot about it.

It seems that the head of talent at Radio 2 at that time liked me, or maybe she just wanted a piece of Virgin and I was the only bit on offer, but she gave us the gig. Michael was thrilled, and a bit smug, as lots of production companies, both in house and independents, had been hoping for the coveted slot.

Chris Whatmough (working at Radio 2 by then also) was ecstatic for me, and took it upon himself to make sure I got a great producer to work with (in addition to Michael's Manchester team), and I started a few weeks later.

Of course, I had to leave Virgin. It seemed beyond ironic for me to leave, rather than be fired! I think they were happy for me, but bizarrely they did see Radio 2 as their competitor at the time. I'd depped for a few *Good Morning Sunday* shows produced by Michael's team (that was fun, using my 'religious skills' once again) and I'd been hauled in to the Virgin management office and told off for 'moonlighting with a competitor'.

I was super-excited to present the Radio 2 early morning show. The hours were brutal, but then I was used to that, and the pay was much better than Virgin, but still, I couldn't manage with one day a week's work. I decided to settle in, and then look around for more. I met with my producers, learned to drive their desk (not dissimilar to the desk at GLR) and marvelled at the joy of having a producer to jack up the various promotions and guests, and help me keep to time, not to mention that there were no commercials to play. What joy!

The week before I started, I was invited to a Radio 2 party. It was some kind of anniversary with a bunch of bands playing at the Café de Paris and I had heard that Steve Wright was starting a show on Radio 2. I'd never met him before, but I recognised him, bounced over and cheekily told him how much of a fan I was and that I was about to join Radio 2 for an early Saturday show, so if he was starting there, he should hire me as a co–presenter! Lo and behold, he did.

We joked about that many times over the years. He said he loved my energy, and once he checked out that I could actually do the gig, it was an easy decision. A few months after I'd started, a female presenter working on another commercial station, sauntered up to him and told him that he should ditch me because she was so much better. He apparently told her, 'I'll make sure that never happens.'

Steve started at Radio 2 with a Saturday afternoon show – beyond tricky because my show finished at 6 a.m. – but the BBC found me a hotel to get a few hours' sleep nearby and I'd get back into the studio for midday. My co-host, Richard Easter, an amazing scriptwriter and comedian, came up with some hilarious features for Steve, including recording jingles as Michael Winner. *'This is Blichael Winna,'* the answerphone would splutter. 'I'm just back from filming *Death Wish 26*, popped into a Michelin star restaurant, had the grilled pike perch…' Years later, the real Michael came in. He'd heard about it and found it hilarious.

The other answerphone message that got a laugh was when Richard would pretend to be an anorak fan. He'd call and say, 'Hi, Steve, I'm your biggest fan… Don't die, Wrighty.' When Steve put a bit of weight on over the years, he would talk about needing to get some exercise, and we'd chirp, 'Don't die, Wrighty!'

Steve's Saturday show lasted only a few weeks before we moved to afternoons. My schedule became five days a week on *Steve Wright in the Afternoon*, and my super-early Saturday a.m. show. Our producer, Paul Rodgers, later king of 6 Music, was – and still is – lovely and naturally hilarious. He missed his vocation as a stand-up, for sure. Paul would effortlessly navigate Steve's moods, which could be a little erratic. Steve was SUCH a perfectionist and there could be a fair bit of snapping at us and at the production team. Mostly, though, we had a lot of fun. Tim Smith joined soon after, and though I knew of him from GLR, we hadn't met before. It was a joy working with Tim: we soon fell into an easy rhythm, and if Steve was being a bit picky, we'd support each other. It was to be the start of 24 years of fun on BBC Radio 2 with *The Big Show*.

Chapter 25
AND AGAIN

When he was about seven months old, we took Sonny to San Francisco. He was the smiliest baby ever, and it quickly struck us that we were seemingly the only couple socialising with a baby in tow. We stayed at our favourite hotel Casa Madrona in Sausalito, just over the Golden Gate Bridge, where he played happily and toddled around in our lovely room, The Artists Lodge, and was a model baby in his buggy when we dined out. But it seemed super-unusual to be out with a young baby. Passers-by would literally stop us in the street and stare at him. 'Is he in the movies?' one couple asked, incredulous; we could only assume that when young couples vacationed, their children stayed with the nanny. In the hotel restaurant the waiter insisted on carrying him into the kitchen to see the chef. We were slightly concerned he'd come back on the serving platter! In another very upmarket restaurant, he was sitting happily on my knee when a couple came over and coo-ed over him, then the woman said, 'You two enjoy your meal, let me take him for a while.' Honestly it was odd!

While I was on that trip, I started to feel a bit dizzy and unwell and couldn't work out what was wrong. I came home to discover I was, in fact, pregnant again. I couldn't have been more delighted, if a bit shocked.

I had been doing the afternoon shows with Steve Wright for a few months when I had to tell him that I was pregnant. I didn't want to take much time off work, but clearly (unlike the Virgin Radio late nights) I wasn't going to be able to be breastfeeding on air! Thankfully they were very happy for me. The only tricky issue was that Steve smoked in the studio. Seems incredible now, doesn't it, people still sat in their offices, smoking like chimneys, guests would sometimes join in too, and the result was a really smoky, sealed room that I was stuck in, for up to five hours, five days a week. I have never been one for confrontation, but I felt nervous for the sake of my baby. I spoke to Paul the producer, and he understood. They never smoked again, and nothing more was ever said. I think the law around indoor smoking came in around then. Thank goodness. Whether you're a smoker or not, how crazy was it that everyone had to breathe that air in enclosed spaces. I worked till Christmas 1999 which gave me a couple of weeks before my baby was due.

During that pregnancy Simon and I had a weekend away and were having breakfast in the hotel when my phone rang. My cab driver said, 'Have you seen the *News of the World*? [then a big-selling Sunday newspaper]. Well, there's a piece in there about you and Simon.'

We knew immediately that it would be Simon's ex up to tricks, and I'd love to know how much she got paid for selling a story! The article headline was 'DJ played singles with married man'. Great headline, to be fair, and it was her account of me 'stealing' her man. Surprisingly, no mention of the fact that, by then, we'd been together for longer than they were married, with one child and another on the way.

For about an hour, we were both pretty upset and worried what might happen as a result of the piece. Then, another call came in from our friend Nikki, who said, 'Hey, what a fantastic photo!' That call completely changed everything – there really is no such thing as bad publicity, especially with a great pic like that!

I did, though, go into Radio 2 the next day with some trepidation. As a general rule the BBC hated their presenters being involved in news stories unless it was about their show, but either no one had seen it or everyone had decided it was deemed too inconsequential to mention – apart from Steve, who merely greeted me as I walked into the studio with: 'Hiya… Home wrecker, are ya?' We all laughed. Tomorrow's chip paper.

It was also during this pregnancy that I caught up with George Michael again. He invited Simon and I to his 'Cowboys and Angels' party to celebrate the new album, and it was, of course, just after his 'coming out' interview, and the shenanigans in the Gents which had preceded it. The invitation said, 'Dress as either a cowboy or an angel. Due to recent events, there will be no public conveniences, so please go before you come.'

While laughing out loud, I was concerned for a moment: I was six months pregnant and constantly needing the loo! Naturally, the toilets were open but almost impossible to get into, due to a long queue of flamboyant angels with wingspans of six feet span. God knows how they manoeuvred into the cubicles. Dressed as a cowboy (I wasn't sure the pregnant fallen angel look would work), I had a long chat with George (who looked very smart but had NOT followed the dress code at all, I was disappointed to see). He spoke about his mum who had passed away not long after the love of his life, Anselmo Feleppa. We spoke about just how cruel cancer can be, about ways of coming to terms with grief and loss. I only wish I'd known then some of the tools I know now; perhaps I could have bent his ear a little more!

For the birth, I wanted to go back to John and Lizzies, and this time I wanted literally all the rides. I met Dr Gowri Motha, an amazing birth guru; I'd heard that she had helped Elle Macpherson, so I reckoned she'd be good enough for me, and we became friends. I loved Gowri's holistic gentle approach and wanted her with me during the birth. By now I was becoming even more interested in holistic living and spirituality, and I started visualising early on that my second baby would be born in the birthing pool. The due date was early January in the year 2000, and there were lots of stories of women who gave birth on Millennium Day, getting free nappies for life. On 31 December 1999 our church threw a New Year's Eve party. I had managed to find an amazing sparkly maternity dress and won their award for the best dressed pregnant woman. The fact that I was the only pregnant woman didn't seem to matter.

I had another long labour. Gowri, bless her, did reiki and reflexology for hours and tried to keep me calm, while the midwives wanted to intervene. I remember calling on every angel, spirit, power for this baby to choose to be born naturally, and suddenly, as if from nowhere, huge contractions started. They draped me over a bean bag, and I screamed, 'But I wanted a water birth!'

'Let's do it, then,' Gowri said, and they heaved me into the pool where a couple of minutes later, Buddy Jackson appeared. Gowri told me afterwards, 'You taught me something today, the power and might of visualisation, I've never seen anyone want something so much … and go after it'.

A bit of a theme for my life, I think!

Simon was at the birth and phoned in to *The Big Show*. Steve announced it on air – so now the world knew!

Life was chaos. When Simon was working away in Newcastle (he was still doing *Byker Grove* for BBC 1), I would literally ricochet from one baby to the next, trying to tandem breastfeed (nightmare) and hold it together. I was determined to be a model mum, so tried to get to antenatal meetings in London or local mums meet-ups. I remember the first time I tried it: Buddy was about two weeks old, and I proudly packed the changing bag with all the paraphernalia for both babies. I got them both in their car seats, strapped in and breathed a sigh of satisfaction. I'd done it. I smiled at myself in the car mirror and with horror realised that, in all the preparations, I had completely forgotten to get dressed! I was wearing pyjama bottoms and a nursing bra! That pretty much summed up life for a good few months!

I went back to *Steve Wright in the Afternoon* when Buddy was about three months old. I was most depressed that while I was off the show one of the guests they interviewed was Eddie Izzard. I was and still am such a fan and had never met him. He often came up in conversation on air, though, and the guys knew how much I loved Eddie. I often joked that I wasn't sure I wanted to meet him; they do say you really shouldn't meet your heroes. Steve and Tim got Eddie to sign his autograph for me with a note that said: 'Thank you for loving me. Eddie X'. I stuck it on the fridge where it stayed for years.

Incredibly when I was off work again for baby number three, Eddie was in again! (I swear they did it on purpose.) Finally, a year or so after that, Eddie was yet again invited to be a guest; I can't recall what he was promoting, but I was working that day. I didn't need to be nervous. He was lovely, and hilarious. I almost cracked a rib laughing. I've never been a fan of stand-up, but Eddie's show was the funniest show I have ever seen, and he didn't disappoint, even in the studio. Afterwards I had a pic taken with him, and I still occasionally post it on Throwback Thursday, when people marvel at our 'matching lipstick'.

Chapter 26
ROCKIN' IT ON *THE BIG SHOW*

Steve Wright in the Afternoon's audience numbers were up to around 9 million listeners, and everyone was happy. Literally every celebrity, actor or author doing the promotional rounds would come on our show, and it was very rare that a guest would turn it down. I've often been asked who my favourite guests were, and aside from Eddie and Chris Martin of Coldplay (because both make my heartbeat faster), that's a tricky one. Steve kept a book and noted down every guest; I so wish I could have had sight of that. I've forgotten so many interviews we did, but some of the highlights for me over the years include Agnetha from ABBA, Tracey Thorn, Goldie Hawn, Andrew Garfield and Susan Sarandon, but there were also guests who weren't big-time celebs but were totally inspirational, such as the late Ken Robinson who gave the ground-breaking TEDx talk 'Do schools kill creativity?'.

We had great celebrity bookers on the team who were great at jacking up the guests, and who usually came into the studio, but sometimes we would go to their showbiz junket if it was a major film release. If you've seen *Notting Hill*, you know about the junket – and they really are like that. You're given an allotted time, and you need to be willing to wait hours, while other seemingly more important publications and TV shows do their interviews first. Then the star typically needs a long lunch break, so you continue to wait, recording device charged up and shovelling in the free coffee and cakes usually supplied. Steve got out of it whenever he could, Tim did the lion's share and sometimes they sent me along. I remember being sent to a hotel room to interview Heather Graham for her role in *The Hangover*. She was very sweet. We talked about Rollergirl in *Boogie Nights* and her family life, and actually had a proper girlie chat. I got to see a preview showing of *The Golden Compass* and then had the opportunity to interview Nicole Kidman and a couple of other actors from the film. It was a massive junket at one of the big hotels and was rammed with 'Arabellas' (as Steve called the PRs) gliding around and looking at clipboards.

Just before I'd gone into the hotel, I'd had a meeting with a brand who wanted to work with me on a natural living project. INIKA was a new Australian brand and had the most fantastic range of organic skincare and cosmetics; this was before natural cosmetics were everywhere, so they were a little ahead of their time. The brand advocate gave me a lovely bag of products to take away and I happened to mention I was going to interview Nicole. She literally paled. 'Oh God,' she said, 'She SO needs our products, please give her this.'

She thrust another goody bag into my hand, stylish black packaging with gold lettering, and off I went.

After waiting an interminable amount of time, I was finally ushered in, bags and all, into the hotel room that had been set up for the filming. 'Audio or visual?' they asked. 'Just audio,' I said and they sat me down, with an empty chair opposite me, which I couldn't help but notice was larger and taller than mine. Very sneaky. One of the Arabellas reminded me that I had a strict 14 minutes and then she would wrap it up: she gestured the hand movement she would make to 'wrap it up', and after a few minutes, they wheeled in Nicole. She was striking, there is no doubt, but she looked fragile and had a slightly ethereal quality. I swear I could tell that under her makeup she had slightly imperfect skin, so how could I not give her the products?

We had a great chat about *The Golden Compass* – her role in it was fantastic and her costumes glorious – and then about her next project, and I actually wrapped exactly 30 seconds before time. As I clicked Stop on the recording device, I passed Nicole the bag I had on my lap. 'I wonder if I could show you this,' I said, 'the brand would love you to have it, it's Australian and organic, beautiful skincare and cosmetics.' The Arabella looked as though she would come over and kill me, but Nicole looked delighted. 'Oh my goodness, thank you,' she said, 'Beautiful packaging, I will definitely try it.'

I think INIKA owe me one for that. I'd settle for their fabulous mascara.

We all went together to interview Russell Crowe, and that one goes down in history as one of the most awkward interviews we ever did. He was just a bit rude, and Wrighty called him out on it; very uncomfortable! Usually, the celebs and stars were well behaved. Of course, we realised that doing the rounds of promo wasn't their favourite bit of the gig, but most of the stars who came into the studio were lovely and Steve treated them all pretty equally, and always in a very relaxed affectionate way.

One of the most fun junkets (and one I've never told anyone about until now) was when I was asked to go and watch the *Sex in the City* film, and then go to the junket and interview four of the stars. I don't know if I am embarrassed or proud to say that I had never seen *Sex in the City*, so it was a steep learning curve, for sure. I knew that my friend Dawn was a huge fan, which was intriguing to me because Dawn was a shamanic healer and about as woo-woo as it's possible to be, but clearly, she had a thing for glamour, and I really needed her expertise when it came to Louboutins so I didn't make a fool of myself. She came to watch the film with me, I quite enjoyed it, and she gave me some great ideas for questions to ask the girls. Then it transpired that I was going to get the opportunity to interview Mr. Big too, and Dawn was beside herself. 'I've asked my angels,' she said, in a matter-of-fact way. 'I know I am meant to meet him.' How could I argue with her angels?

I told her to meet me at the hotel, but I couldn't guarantee she would be able to come in with me. Of course I didn't mention it to the producers of our show, they didn't need to know, and in any case most of the interviewers had assistants to hold their equipment. I had quite an annoying recording device and I practised several times to ensure I got it right, so having a second pair of eyes on it was useful. We rocked up to the production desk. 'Janey and Dawn from Steve Wright's show,' we said, and they waved us through. We interviewed the girls individually: Sarah Jessica Parker was lovely. (She blew my socks off in her role in the 2005 film *The Family Stone*); Kim Cattrall looked a little exhausted, bless her; and Kristin Davis was quiet. With job done, Dawn and I sat in the green room drinking yet more coffee while we waited to be called in to chat to Chris Noth.

He was charming. I could feel Dawn by my side, practically shaking from being so close to her hero, and we did a great interview where he cracked some jokes and shared some good soundbites. We got back into the green room, and I checked the device. It hadn't recorded. I put the headphones on, rewound, and there was the interview with the girls, then …silence.

On my God! In all my years of doing professional radio I had never cocked up like that, and to this day I don't know how it happened. I was convinced – and so was Dawn – that we had pressed it into record mode. I went cold, it was simply not going to be OK to go back to the studio with half a tale; Wrighty would be furious. I was seriously panicking. I asked Dawn if she could call upon her angels one more time as I gushingly begged whoever was at the production desk to let us have just five more minutes, as our device hadn't worked. I was convinced I'd get the Arabella stare, and they'd simply say: 'No way!', but clearly Dawn's higher powers seemed to kick in and they were charming. 'Of course Chris won't mind, he will think it's funny,' they said. And incredibly, we did it all again, in Record mode this time, as if the first time had simply been a practice run.

Dawn was elated, but not at all surprised. 'I think I manifested it,' she said. 'Angels saw to it that I got to meet Chris Noth, not once but twice!'

The other notable junket for me was when I was sent to interview Julia Roberts for *Eat, Pray, Love*. To say I adored that film was an understatement. I had already devoured the book, so watching the film felt like a treat and she was, in my opinion, perfect in the role.

I rocked up at the hotel and they told me to go into one of the suites and wait. I opened the door, into a huge room with big sofas, and there was just one girl sitting with her feet up on the sofa. That was most unusual for the Arabellas, as they usually were on their heels, and you rarely saw them off guard. 'I'm Janey from Radio 2,' I said to the back of her head, and she spun round and gave me the most dazzling smile I've ever seen in real life. 'Hi, I'm Julia,' she said. 'I LOVE your skirt.' It was a pretty cool skirt to be fair, with pictures of Frida Kahlo, made for me by my very talented designer friend Rosi. 'Thank you,' I said, and then the Arabella came in, looking shocked that we'd already met and hit it off, and the interview began. Julia was entirely 'normal', literally like a regular girl, no starriness, or ethereal replicant vibe, just someone I would definitely be friends with, in another life.

The time Bono came into the show was memorable. I was excited to meet him. U2 had been intrinsic in my musical life. I first saw them at Hammersmith Apollo supported by The Alarm in 1983, and Bono was a 'Greenbelt icon'. I asked him to say Hi to Pete (known as Willy) Williams who I'd known from my early twenties (one of the 'two Petes'), and now the group's long-time lighting designer. Bono said, 'Come and surprise him, it's his birthday tomorrow and we're going give a shout out at the gig, you can hop on our private plane, no worries.'

So I flew to the Sheffield Don Valley Stadium on 20 August 2009, as part of their U2 360° Tour, got reunited with Pete and had a fantastic time, flew back to Luton airport, and got whisked home in a limo. Honestly, how the other half live!

An old muso mate of mine was wide eyed: 'Did you join the mile high club in their learjet?' he asked. Certainly not! It was all extremely conservative. Bono and his wife flew separately, and I lounged demurely across from The Edge, drinking earl grey tea and being offered smoked salmon canapes from the immaculately dressed 1950's style stewardesses.

Rock 'n' Roll!

Chapter 27
THE BIG APPLE... LOVE SONGS... AND MORE GUESTS

Steve loved going to the USA. He had friends and family there and would sometimes go straight after the show on a Friday and come back on the red-eye in time for the show on Monday. He had a fascination with drug store medication that you could buy in the US but not here, and he would regularly bring back Excedrin – good for headaches and colds apparently – and dole them out to any celeb who came in complaining of a cold or a headache! It became a bit of a standing joke that Wrighty had a little pharmacy in his desk drawer!

We took *The Big Show* to the USA in 2001. We stayed in the Tribeca area of New York, a few months before 9/11, and with only about five days in the city, we had a packed schedule. The producers did a good job of jacking up some interesting guests. First up was Wall Street, where our contact, money expert Alvin Hall, had arranged a tour of the building. We recorded on the actual floor with traders shouting: 'Sell!' all around us. It really was like something from a film. We filmed at the diner made famous (or infamous) by that scene from *When Harry Met Sally* – 'I'll have what's she's having'. Katz's Delicatessen is on the Lower East Side, and they looked after us with huge pastrami sandwiches, and kept on refilling the black coffee cups. Amazingly, we somehow got to interview Rudy Giuliani going through a ridiculous amount of security so that the whole team were led into a huge office with a view over the city.

We had some evening assignments too. Sadly, with times clashing, we had to split up. Producer Paul and I went to Madison Square Gardens to see Michael Flatley's *Riverdance*. Steve was meant to be with us too, but somehow managed to arrive late and still get in, we know not how! It's not my kind of thing at all, and Paul and I kept each other entertained with an unrepeatable commentary throughout. We were quite jealous of Steve, who had managed to not have to sit through it all, but still rocked up backstage to do the interviews. There were lots of film crews there, and we were concerned that we'd be there most of the night. Steve, as ever, was super-efficient and didn't want to be kept waiting. 'Could you wheel in the little jigger?' he said to one of the 'gliders', 'I'm a very busy man.'

She thought it so hilarious, she said yes, and brought Michael into a round of applause from the adoring ensemble of press and TV operatives, leading him straight over to our table where we got to do the interview and get out of there fast.

You can imagine how much we loved it when we interviewed Sean Lock some months later for his new tour. 'No Flatley, *I* am the Lord of the Dance!'

When Steve went away on one of his solo US trips, there was the not inconsequential issue of the volcanic eruptions in Iceland, resulting in the ash cloud that grounded airline travel. (Seems nothing now after the Covid era, but at the time it was monumental.) It became apparent that Steve couldn't get back to the UK in time to do his *Sunday Love Songs* show, so he called me and asked if I'd sit in for him. I was delighted, who wouldn't be? I loved that show and was honoured to be asked. *Love Songs* was Steve's creation, and he told me that he had called the management and said he wanted me to dep the show.

That was the beginning of a long period where I always sat in for Steve on that show. It really was a joy to do, because in addition to having the excuse of playing the most schmaltzy, fabulous, tear-jerking tracks, it was the simplest format ever: play tracks and read out listeners' letters. These weren't just dedications: 'Play a track for my husband'; we wanted details, and details we got! Some of the letters actually made me cry, and I had to brace myself to read them out on air without falling apart. If for one second you had thought romance was dead, you simply had to listen to an episode.

One of the features on the show was trying to reunite people, and there was nothing more joyful than hearing some weeks after broadcast that old friends or lovers had met up, after having been lost to each other, sometimes for decades.

I had a fantastic run of depping *Love Songs*, but after a few years the management decided they needed celebs, so whenever Steve was away, they put a TV presenter in his place. Steve often told me he had asked for me to continue doing it, but you can't argue with the big guys. I was always so grateful that he'd given me a leg-up, though; he was that kind of guy. If he could do something to make your life better, he would.

* * *

It never failed to entertain when a star's PR team would lay down the law about what questions could or couldn't be asked on *Steve Wright in the Afternoon.* That was a red rag to Steve. Buzz Aldrin's people said: 'No questions about the moon.' *What?* 'No questions about the Beatles' was the instruction for George Harrison's wife (who had written a book). Some may remember the news reports of an irate Diana Ross being searched by security at Heathrow. 'Don't mention the airport,' someone from her overlarge entourage ordered. Of course, Steve's first question was: 'What was all that at the airport, then?' Diana laughed. That was often the case: the celeb's 'people' were sometimes more uptight than the stars themselves.

I think the only obnoxious interviewee we had was James Hewitt. He'd written a book, and obviously we were going to ask him about Diana. He was irritated from the off because it was clear we hadn't read his book cover to cover. Sounds fair enough, but it was typical to be given a book the night before the interview if we were lucky, and then it was a case of scanning the book, picking out the interesting topics and asking the questions that the listeners – who, after all hadn't read it either but might be persuaded to buy it – would want to know. But James snapped at us and called us unprofessional or some such, and Wrighty had very little time for him. We carried on with the interview, allowing him to dig himself into a hole as it came across just how unlikable he was. Off air, Steve tried to give him some advice about how to do himself some favours in these kinds of situations. I don't think he listened.

There were other guests with whom we had a sort of love-hate relationship, Wrighty always made jokes about them, and some of the chat off air would have definitely made headlines. There were some celebs he absolutely detested, but of course that didn't come across on air. Part of the fun was watching a few self-centred celebs and politicians lap up the seeming adoration, knowing that we would be calling them every name under the sun after they'd left. Everything seemed like childish fun, to be honest.

One celeb, who stopped by fairly regularly, genuinely thought he was one of Steve best mates: We would marvel at why he hadn't clocked that Steve enjoyed making fun of him On one occasion when he was due in for a chat, we kept him waiting in the green room for a few minutes, then Steve pressed the talk button that connected to the control room, which was the interconnecting room between the green room area and our soundproofed studio. From where Tim and I sat in our studio we had sight of the green room door through the glass, and to our horror just as Steve pressed the talkback button and said: 'Go on, then, wheel in the muppet...' in walked the celeb, hearing every word! Tim and exchanged a look of horror and as he burst through the studio door, Wrighty had the grace to look shocked. Fortunately, the celeb was laughing. 'Muppet yourself, Wrighty.' he said.

One recurring gag we had was Steve's deliberate mispronunciation of words, *skellington* being one of his favourites (Dr Hilary Jones had given him a real full-size skeleton as a birthday present). Another was Genius – pronounced 'gun-eye-us'. Sometimes 'Outraged from Tunbridge Wells' would write in, unimpressed at the BBC's inability to correctly pronounce the Queen's English. Wrighty called pretty much everyone 'Matey boy', so in conversation, he'd say: 'Did you see that piece about matey boy?' and somehow either Tim or I would be able to read his mind and know exactly which matey boy he was referring to!

Another running joke when the mics were off was about celebs having 'work done' – 'sugary', Steve called it, and he was very unimpressed when celebs came in having clearly just topped up the Botox. 'Don't ever do that s—t, Janey,' he used to say, and I'd tell him I had no intention. 'I'm not looking forward to looking old, though,' I said. 'I know you'll be merciless.' 'Definitely,' he assured me, 'I will tell you the minute you go hag.' We were interviewing one very well-known but much older woman one time, and his line was 'Wheel in the faded icon'. How Tim and I managed to keep a straight face as she walked in, I can't imagine. He missed his vocation as a comedian for sure, but while his quips might have sounded a bit scathing, he was kind, and it was all good-hearted fun.

Politicians often came by the show too, and it was then that we saw a different side to Steve. He would remain friendly and approachable, but he always gave them hard-hitting questions. Initially many thought they were stopping by our studio for light relief after the stress of *Question Time*, but Steve would often ask them the tricky stuff, and it was clear he had a journalistic background and wasn't going to let them off lightly.

* * *

We loved it when TV chefs came in, usually to promote a new book. Jamie Oliver would always bring in a Tupperware box with treats for us, and I remember one day when he was working on the wholesome school meals project (remember that?) we spoke about it on air, but when the mics were turned off, he told us some of the heartbreaking stories about the lack of nutrition for some of the children he had encountered. He was on the verge of tears. He really went up in my estimation; no way was he doing that for publicity. Nigella Lawson was just lovely too; she always came bearing goods, usually something involving chocolate which was very difficult to eat when we were talking.

Gordon Ramsay, another favourite guest, rarely brought food, but what he did bring was his acerbic wit. He was very funny. Steve would make a comment about not being an especially good cook, and Gordon would retort, 'That's because you've got sausage fingers, lose some weight!' On one occasion when he came in, I'd just moved into my new home with a Rayburn AGA, and I had no idea how to use it. 'What do you recommend?' I asked him, hoping for some tips on baking and roasting. 'Shove some f—g dried flowers in it and buy a gas cooker' was his reply. He was right, to be fair. Although I loved the look of the AGA, and it kept the kitchen warm, we couldn't fry an egg properly for six years and then it completely died. One time Gordon came in, his wife Tania had been in a few days before, to promote her own recipe book. It was lying around on the desk as he arrived. 'FFS,' he sighed …I think he was joking. The other chef I loved interviewing was Jack Monroe (of *A Girl Called Jack*). She brought in a whole meal, and it was delicious!

Talking of chefs, Tim and I got to feature on *Ready Steady Cook*. I felt properly nervous, as I genuinely struggle with cooking, but they assured us it would be fine. The producers chat to you before the recording and you agree the kinds of foods you like, which they then bring in. With our assistance, the celebrity chefs make a meal, using those same ingredients. When we arrived at the studio, we realised that our celeb chefs genuinely had not had sight of the ingredients until we were literally live on the set! I couldn't believe it; I was with Ainsley Harriott and he was hilarious. He took a quick look at the collection of ingredients I'd suggested and started getting to work on making garlic flat-breads and a wonderful risotto. 'Chop these, Janey,' he said, passing me a knife and some coriander and parsley. I carefully started chopping and he fell about laughing at my lack of technique. 'Can you go a bit faster, it's only a 20-minute slot!' he said. We had a huge laugh, but sadly Tim won. I think it was because he'd opted for a meat dish – and to be fair, it did look good. The dish created by Ainsley, though, was one of the tastiest things I've ever had. As the show was coming to an end, they said: 'Tuck in', so the camera closed in for some close-ups of us tasting the food, and then the cameras stayed on us as the credits rolled. No one knew that I was almost three months pregnant and was at the stage where I was starving, and this food was unreal! I couldn't stop eating it, while Tim was just delicately having a little taste. I didn't know that they'd give us the food to finish in the green room, and I couldn't stop. When I watched the show back, I was mortified; I can be seen in glorious technicolour shovelling food in like I hadn't eaten for a week as the credits rolled. Ainsley thought it was extremely amusing. I still have the bright red *Ready Steady Cook* apron signed by Ainsley.

Years later, Tim and I were invited back on telly as a duo for *Celebrity Antiques Road Trip*. Again, I was nervous, antiques not being my thing, but again, I was assured the experts would help. I partnered with David Harper, who was so knowledgeable and friendly, and it was a well-oiled machine as productions go. The first day of filming saw Tim and I driving along in a beautiful vintage Aston Martin, and making a few references to Steve, who of course had not wanted to be involved. Steve was constantly offered things like that: TV slots, all the reality shows, I'm a Celebrity – Get me out of here, *Big Brother* – I think he turned down just about everything. His heart was always and only in radio.

For *Antiques Road Trip*, Tim and I rocked up to some antiques shops where the owners had been primed, but they didn't give us any special treatment. David told me just to browse and find some things that caught my eye. I really enjoyed the process. We had such a laugh as he saw me looking at a small silver gong. 'What do you like about that?' he asked. 'Thinking you'd like to use it to call the kids to dinner?' I said, 'No, I wish it were bigger, so it could be used for a gong bath.' 'What?' he said, 'do you get wet?'

It made for good TV, and in fact the gong went for a decent amount of money. On the second day of filming, in another fab old motor with David driving (I declined), we were going uphill on a country road when the engine literally spluttered and died. I really thought that was it, and our schedule was trashed for the day, but amazingly their on-team mechanic fixed it effortlessly and we were off again in no time. That surely would not happen with a modern car – I mean the easy fixing bit, not the breakdown. The final day of filming was the auction. My items, especially the gong and an unusual African statue I'd found, did quite well, but my final purchases which were original street signs, went for less than I'd paid for them. *Ouch*. Tim, however, got a rather more conventional antique card table, which had caused much hilarity being covered by a bin bag to hide it as it stuck out of the top of the vintage car. It went for a decent amount, and so Tim won. Again. Only by 20 quid, though

I can't talk about the Radio 2 years without mentioning *Children in Need*. It became such a thing every year: Pudsey Bear would be lurking in the green room and we had to do all kinds of different stuff on the auction days. Steve would always get stressed that something would go wrong. If it did, no one noticed. We were always amazed by how much money was raised. By far the most memorable was the year that Rylan Clark did a 24-hour singathon. Of course, he got some breaks and time went fast when lots of amazing celebs came by. I was offered the opportunity to duet with Rylan, so we did Elton John and Kiki Dee's 'Don't Go Breaking My Heart', and as we finished the end lines, I realised that Nicole Scherzinger had been looking on. 'You're really good,' she said, and Rylan agreed it was 'very special'.

That was also the occasion when I got 'rickrolled'. I couldn't believe that in all my years hanging around studios, even working with Stock, Aitken and Waterman I hadn't met Rick Astley before. So, I finally did.

Kelsey Grammer came to *The Big Show*

Chapter 28
HOME, SWEET HOME

By 2001 the big ultra-modern home no longer seemed to work. The boys were toddlers, and we had one too many stressful scenarios near the swimming pool, which was far too big for the size for the garden. It was time for an old brown house rather than a flashy new white one. We put the house on the market, got a sale, and looked for something to rent while we decided what we wanted to buy next. After a tip-off from one of the kids' kindergarten teachers, we found a kooky old house on three floors in Old Hatfield which had once been a department store. You could still see the word *Haberdashery* on the original staircase.

I will always remember sitting on my sofa at Brookmans Park, feeding Buddy when Simon rang me and told me to put the TV on. There were scenes of planes going into the World Trade Centre, and it changed everything. The effects are still rippling out. Just a few weeks later our buyers dropped out. 'Market instability,' they said. But we just wanted out, so we moved anyway, and rented out the Brookmans Park house.

That was a happy period for a while – renting and renting. The house in Old Hatfield was definitely not right for us to stay in for long, but it got us into the area, and we loved it.

A few months later, the same teacher told us of a big old Georgian town house, The Garden House. It was in the same street, but at the top, near the entrance to Hatfield House, a stately mansion where Queen Elizabeth I lived for a while. We walked up the street and saw that bright blue door – and I knew. It was empty, but we walked around the back, tiptoed over the gravel and into an overgrown orchard. Wild garlic! OMG. We ventured into a long-walled garden and peeked into the house. It had not been cared for, and looked in a sorry state, but I knew instantly that I loved it and wanted to live there. I rang the estate office and got the distinct impression that they were planning to do it up a bit, then get big bucks from a corporate let. My teacher freind suggested I write a personal letter to one of the estate managers, and I figured I had nothing to lose. I worked hard on that letter. It went along the lines of:

> *We would love to be part of this community and have a family who would cherish this family home....* I remember adding: *We hear of people discovering their dream home, this is most definitely ours, I so hope you will be able to consider making my dream a reality.*

I posted the letter at 4.45 p.m., and I remember clearly sending a little wish as I popped it into the letter box. The very next morning at 9.30 a.m., I got a call from the estate office saying, *Thank you for your letter.* (How had it got there that fast?) *Let's meet at the house, does tomorrow suit?*

The rent was extortionate, but we loved that house – the perfect place for our brood, and we had very different, but still awesome parties in the orchard and huge garden.

Chapter 29
WEDDING BELLS

That spring, in the grounds of Hatfield Park, Simon asked me to marry him and I was overjoyed. I think I had just accepted that I'd never be married: his experience had been so painful, and I didn't think he'd want to go there, but he actually got down on one knee (well, on a tree stump) and of course I said yes. Initially we wanted to get married at the gorgeous St. Etheldreda's Church directly opposite the Garden House, so we arranged to speak to the vicar. We knew that Simon having been married before could be an issue, and that this was at the discretion of each individual church and vicar. He looked genuinely disappointed but said he couldn't consider it. 'Why?' we asked. 'We're local, part of the community, kids in the Sunday club, etc.,' I explained something of my Christian past, and that I even had a 'license' to serve communion from the Bishop of London. (Ought to count didn't it!) He shook his head and explained that, if he married us, it would send a message: Simon was getting a second chance, and this would, quite frankly, annoy those members of the congregation who because of their faith, had stuck with their marriages despite being unhappy.

Dave Tomlinson, the vicar at St Luke's in London, had no such qualms and was delighted to marry us. We got married that summer, and Sonny and Buddy, after much wrangling and dressed in matching red shorts suits, looked ultra-cute. Gerberas were everywhere, and the whole vibe was natural and colourful. When the vicar said: 'I now pronounce you man and wife', Buddy, then two and a half, walked up and stood between us holding a Silver Star balloon. The whole church rang with the sound *'Ahh'*.

Everyone hightailed out to Hertfordshire for our reception at the house in Brookmans Park, which we had managed to reclaim at the last minute from the tenants from hell. To this day I don't know what went down there, but boy, they were a nightmare! The woman threatened not to get out when the tenancy ended, and then decided she would but would need to be put up in a hotel at our expense. I rang her once and pleaded with her. It was like talking to a plank. We were desperate, so we agreed, but just as we were arranging it, we got a call from our neighbour in Brookmans Park. 'They're moving out,' he said, 'There is a big truck loading up.' That was all we needed to know. We pulled the hotel deal. She was clearly too stupid to realise our neighbours might tell us they'd already gone. We rocked up at the house, changed the locks, cleared the horrible amount of rubbish they'd left and swallowed the fact that they owed us money. I've since heard of landlords who've had a much worse time.

It was great fun having the wedding reception back in the big white house. It was a beautiful day, and several people jumped in the pool before the bands played. We had Barry Upton's' band Hotpantz A Go Go (you can imagine what they were like from the name) and to counter the pop tartness, we also had Simon's long-time friend Billy Jenkins, and band. Billy was hysterically entertaining. I always hated jazz, but Billy took the piss out of it, despite being an incredibly talented jazz guitarist.

We were far too full-on to have a honeymoon, but Fiona, who was our 'mothers help' took the kids to her house and we got one night in a hotel. We chose Pendley Manor in Tring, and my overriding memory is waking up around 6 a.m. to the sound of a weird screaming. I bolted upright wondering which child was crying, only to realise it was the peacocks strutting around the grounds. Beautiful – but very noisy.

Back at the Garden House, we now had the space with a lovely attic room, so an au pair, Oana, joined us from Romania. She was just perfect: I am so grateful to her, and the kids still talk about her now.

Chapter 30
SCHOOL'S OUT

We decided to home educate. What home educating really means is joining with a whole community of other home educators, so the kids would go to different places on different days. It took a lot of organisation but somehow it worked. A couple of days a week, they attended a small school called NatureKids. Felicity Evans, now an author and parenting consultant, was the leading light. Her basic theory is that if enough time is spent in nature, children will then engage their brain. The boys loved it: they'd climb a tree, build a den, and then maybe do a page or two of maths. They would be given a home-cooked meal, then go sailing, horse riding, or whatever activity she could jack up. It was magical.

I found out I was pregnant again in early January 2003, and this one was planned. When I was around seven months, my father was taken into hospital, he had developed a raging infection during that extremely hot summer, where the UK had seen temperatures in the 40s. I was the size of a house and literally sweltering, and when I rang the hospital to see how he was, I am ashamed to say, I really didn't want to make the trip to Bournemouth to see him.

The nurse told me they'd administered strong antibiotics. 'I'll be very surprised if they don't kick in quickly,' she said reassuringly. They didn't. My father, who also had a mental illness of sorts which perhaps manifested as hypochondria, had taken so many courses of antibiotics over the years that when he really needed them, they didn't work. The young nurse called me back late one night. 'I can't understand why he isn't responding to the antibiotics,' she said. I told her sadly, that if she read his full notes, she might understand why. 'It might be best if you come,' she said. We called Phil, who in addition to being the best piano player ever, was our only 'free' childcare, and he drove straight over to be there for the kids while Simon and I fled to Bournemouth.

We arrived at the hospital at about 5 a.m. The nurse said, 'He's just in that room there'. My heart lifted as I thought perhaps, he had picked up a bit. We quietly opened the door and stood over him. He was dead. In the moments while my brain tried to make sense of it, the nurse realised what a catastrophic error she had made. She burst into the room saying: 'You didn't know, I'm so sorry. I thought someone had called you, …there is a process for complaints.' 'It's OK,' I said. Suing the hospital wouldn't bring him back. My mum's way of handling the shock was not ideal. She simply (we realised later) stopped taking her medication and lurched into a terrible series of bipolar highs (as they're commonly known). It's too painful to document some of the stuff that went down in those first few years after my dad died, but it was pretty awful. Thankfully Mum lived in assisted housing with wardens on site who could check in from time to time, but her typical behaviour when she left behind her medication was to go wandering off, walking for miles, with no money or food. She had to be sectioned a few times, and it was unbelievably sad and very stressful.

One happier memory from that pregnancy, though, was getting a call from Barry Upton. The previous year I'd sung on some tracks he was doing with Dean Friedman. Who doesn't love Dean? One was a remake of 'Lucky Stars', a more dancey version (I know, the audacity messing with a classic!) and suddenly it had been picked up and we were being invited to do *Top of the Pops 2*.

Dean asked me if I'd sing with him on *TOP2*. I said, *I'd love to, the only slight snag being that I'm eight months pregnant, so will he be OK with me having a bump?* I don't think he'd ever been asked that before, and he seemed very concerned that it would be an issue, but I assured him I'd be fine.

I wore my lovely sparkly maternity dress and flares, and we were seated on high stools and you could barely notice the bump. The camera guys were all joking about needing hot towels and boiling water, but I knew it was fine. It's fun looking back at that video now. A few years ago, Dean came to the UK for a tour and asked me to sing with him. I rocked up at several venues, duetted on 'Lucky Stars' (the original, not Barry's version!) much to the chagrin of the audience who just wanted to sing those bits themselves! His solo shows, which he is still doing around the world as I write this, are just great, intimate and fun. He includes all the hits and there are at least two that make you cry.

* * *

Baby number three, Rocky, came along in October that year. Once again, Simon called into the show and Steve announced the birth on air. There was a lot to manage.

Our au pair Oana was fantastic: I was working just three days a week at the BBC and Simon was full-on in our home studio. He had lots of work for TV companies doing signature tunes, and became known as Mr Quiz, doing all the music for programmes such as *Catchphrase*, *Jeopardy* and *Crosswits*.

Rocky was a force to be reckoned with from Day One. He was adored by Oana (not so much by his older brothers), but of course he changed the dynamic of our little family forever. Not much longer after that it was to change again, but before baby number four came, I found I had an emerging second career.

Chapter 31
A NEW CHAPTER

Alongside the guests and the factoids on *The Big Show*, we had our 'talky bits': Steve would read bits of the day's news, and Tim and I would bring other interesting stories we'd come across. We would focus on any special occasions, anything relatable that was going on. Those stories often led to chats about the things going on in our personal lives. Tim got a bit typecast as being a 'sad and lonely golfer' (although we had to phase that one out when he met and married Leone) while I was down as the 'slightly woo-woo earth mother'. If there were ever stories around food, I'd obviously want to share my views on natural living, choosing organic, unprocessed, grass-fed, etc. If there were stories around health and wellbeing, I'd have a view; anything linked to parenting, and I'd be advocating for the most natural approach. Steve found some of my ideas just too 'out there' and would fade the mic down and laugh at me as I spoke about natural deodorants, Hopi ear candles, shamanic healing, essential oils, etc. It all made for good radio, though, and of course I was regularly inundated with emails or messages from listeners saying, *Don't let those guys take the mickey, I'd love to know whether there really is natural deo that work* or *How can I get my whites white without chemical detergent?* I found myself replying to hundreds of emails, sharing tips and info.

One day I got an email from a publisher called Caroline, who asked if I'd thought about writing a book on my tips and ideas around holistic living. I laughed and said I hadn't considered it. Caroline drove to Hertfordshire from Wales and took me out to lunch. She said she had heard me talk so much about natural products and complementary medicine over the years and she guessed that lots of listeners were genuinely interested. 'I'm not a writer,' I said, and she simply replied: 'Don't worry, you've clearly got a passion, you have enthusiasm. If you really can't write well, we can help.'

It turned out I could write, and I started on the process of writing my first book *Imperfectly Natural Woman*. I am, to this day, so glad that I chose that title. I didn't want to claim to be holier than thou, and in the book, I say: *Start where you're at, you may not get everything right, but you can do the bits you can.*

Once I began writing, I found I had a lot to share. I wrote about the emerging new natural cosmetics and skincare, organic haircare, and bath-time bliss. I researched a lot for the chapters on eco paints and natural cleaning products, and of course there was a lot on food and supplements, which I titled 'Natural Kitchen'. There was a chapter on women's stuff (many a guy has told me he started on that chapter) and throughout the book I recommended brands, products and services that I had come across over the years.

The book was due to be released in October 2005, but soon after meeting Caroline and getting started on the book, I found out that I was pregnant again and baby number four was due in September. We put the date of the book back till early 2006 and I set about navigating another baby. I think that by now Steve and the BBC were getting used to me disappearing to have babies, and this time, I did recognise that I might have to take a bit longer off work, with pregnancy, writing a book and already having three young children to contend with. The surprise was, I found I loved writing. Sadly, a bit too much: I wasn't terribly disciplined and ended up writing over 100,000 words when we needed only 70,000. That was a lesson!

In September 2005, Simon and I took off to John and Lizzies for the fourth and final time. The birth was easier, and thankfully the baby was born in water again. They do say when you've had three boys, the likelihood to continue is strong, and when baby number four floated up in the water, and the midwife said: 'You have a girl', I simply didn't believe them.

After Lulu's birth I came the closest ever to understanding postnatal depression. I felt so blessed and loved her, but the exhaustion and the sense of overwhelm was something I couldn't have imagined. I remember reading about a mother who had worried that she might have run out of unconditional love, that her quota might have been used up by the first two or three children – but somehow it expands. I think I was in that phase of trying to adjust to more overwhelming love and responsibility. Simon was full-on too: he absolutely pulled his weight with the kids, but there was just nothing left over for caring for ourselves. Gowri had often told me that in an ideal world new mums had a golden period where they could stay in bed nursing their baby for one month, while their extended family and community brought meals and cared for them. *Wow*. Before I

In my messy office

descended into depression, I found the wherewithal to call a therapist I'd met some years earlier. She came over, gave me a gentle massage, some kind of energy healing and told me to remember to take care of myself too.

One of the most memorable presents I received during that time was when Lulu was a couple of months old. One of my friends, Rowan, who had her children young, turned up with a huge meal and said, 'You and Simon can go out for a few hours, enjoy yourself. I will stay with all the children, off you go.' It was a weird experience, putting make-up on and a dress that I wouldn't have been able to breastfeed in, but once we got in the car, we realised we were both so knackered, we just had a sleep!

* * *

Imperfectly Natural Woman was published in March 2006, and I was very proud of my first book. The small publisher had made it look fantastic with colour pics and endorsements from Dr Hilary Jones and Lynne Franks, and I told my friends and family to buy it at their local bookshop (there were still quite a few in those days). Except they couldn't, no stores stocked it, so unless it was ordered in, it was nowhere to be found. I just hadn't realised that unless you are mega-famous or published by a big publisher, your book is rarely stocked. The publisher agreed we needed more PR, so we split the cost of a PR agent (madly expensive) who did a press release and apparently wrote to all their media contacts. Nothing, zilch, zip. I was absolutely gutted. My life's work in that 70,000-word book, all my tips and recommendations, but apart from some sales via Amazon, no one could buy it and it seemed no one was interested. A few really good reviews came in, but I simply couldn't accept that it would just fizzle out. I decided to take it into my own hands and hustle to get myself out there. Because it was the BBC, my book couldn't be mentioned on the show at all, which was frustrating, but I did give a book to Johnnie Walker's producer, and she booked me onto his *Drivetime* show.

I'd always been a fan of Johnnie's. I think I cited him once years ago as my favourite radio presenter, so I was very excited to be interviewed by him. He was very health-conscious at the time and fascinated by the contents of my book. We spent that hour discussing so many topics, from natural skincare, deodorants, organic food and therapies to how to be more eco-friendly by focusing on natural health and wellbeing first. The production team were incredulous: they had a huge number of calls during the show, the phone lines literally ringing off the hook, with people wanting to ask questions and get recommendations, or just say how much they'd enjoyed the interview.

The following day, Caroline my publisher called. 'You're Number 1,' she said. 'On what?' I asked. I had no idea what she meant, but it turned out the book had hit the main Amazon bestsellers list overnight, knocking Dan Brown's *Da Vinci Code* off the top spot. 'You're kidding me! What does that actually mean?' I asked. She said it meant that suddenly every Waterstones in the UK wanted loads of copies, where a few days previously they weren't interested in stocking any. It meant that suddenly journalists wanted to interview me, the book was serialised in a mainstream newspaper, I was invited to do book signings and events, and suddenly a huge number of people joined my little forum (this was before the days of Facebook groups).

I couldn't have known exactly how much that book was about to change the course of my life. Suddenly my woo-woo ideas, my earth mother, eco and natural approach was valued, and I was very grateful that I knew I'd made it accessible and realistic. The publisher sent Johnnie a huge box of something as a thank you, probably a case of Johnnie Walker!

For the next couple of weeks, I was insanely busy replying personally to emails, trying to keep up my forum, setting up a website to add info about recommended products, and trying to sort out childcare so that I could go and give talks around the UK. We put a book tour in place, and several people started to ask me why I wasn't on commission for the many products I was recommending. If truth be told, I had never considered it. Just like I hadn't considered myself a writer, I also hadn't thought of being 'in business' and didn't know an affiliate deal from a business plan. One day, I bumped into Johnnie at the BBC. He told me he had just been to a homeopathic pharmacy in Marylebone. 'I tried to buy some of a natural cough medicine you recommended in the book,' he said, 'but they're all sold out. In fact, they said that a few products had literally been flying off the shelves for a few weeks and they can't understand it. I told them why,' he added. 'I told them it's the power of being *Janey*'d.' I laughed and said it wouldn't have happened without the exposure on his show.

And that was where my second career started. I had yet another steep learning curve, putting together a recommendations' website where, rather than take commissions on products, I offered brand collaborations to companies whose products I endorsed, and they paid a small amount of money to be featured on the website. I still wrote about masses of brands who have never to this day paid anything, but some of the brands I wrote about in my first book, have done brand collaborations and entered my yearly awards for natural products and services. I quickly built a list of engaged people who wanted to know about the latest products and therapies I'd discovered, and for a while I was in demand for talks, Mind Body Spirit shows and events.

I did some lovely events during that period, a tour of bookshops in Wales and the north of England, and a whole bunch of radio stations; it was fun going back to some of the local stations I'd been to with the records. Simon and I also had one fabulous trip to Loch Lomond to a wonderful independent bookshop right by the shore. They put us up in a funky hotel and offered us a whisky tour. I was drinking copious amounts of wine at that time, and thankfully hadn't gone down the slippery slope of spirits, but it was a wonderful trip.

The book had been out and flying high for a few months when I got an email from a big-time literary agent. 'Congratulations on your recent success,' they said. 'Would you like to meet us for a chat?' I thought: *Why not?* and off I went to meet the lovely Euan. He was very complimentary about the book, delighted that I had no representation, and explained to me that he could almost certainly get me a great publishing deal for my next book. I was dubious about not staying with my current publisher, but I knew they could be limited in their reach, so I drafted a proposal for an all-singing, all-dancing A–Z of holistic living and Euan touted it to a few publishers. I had meetings with three of them, then they made offers. One offer came in with a little sweetener in the form of a case of organic wine and high quality 70 per cent chocolate – how could I refuse?

The money offered to me by one major publishing house was ridiculous, and I just couldn't turn it down. I'm not a lover of conflict, so letting down the publisher who had literally got me started was tough to say the least, and they did not take it well – but it happens all the time in the publishing world, so I had to put my big girl pants on and ask to be released from my deal.

It felt very exciting. The new editor was so enthusiastic about my book: the stuff I spoke about was so on trend, she said, you are going to be the next Gwyneth Paltrow but for 'real women'. I liked that, it felt good. But when they announced in a press release the details of signing me in the publishing press, the original publishing house was not happy and threatened a lawsuit. Euan thought it would blow over. 'They can't have jurisdiction over you,' he said. The argument was that the new title would stop *Imperfectly Natural Woman* from selling because it would include some similar topics. But books have a natural life, and then readers want the sequel, and just because Jamie Oliver, say, signs to a different publisher, he can't never do a shepherd's pie again!

It all got messy, and I was feeling increasingly upset and stressed. I spoke to a barrister who said: it was my intellectual property, and so long as I didn't simply lift the original book (obviously), the new material could of course contain the same themes because that was my topic as an author. Just as it was all reaching a head, the editor of the new publishing house who had signed me went off on maternity leave, and I was assigned a different editor who I don't think 'got' what I did. She did not want a fight on her hands during her temporary job, so she suggested I abandon the A–Z idea, and make the first book about natural parenting instead, which would be different enough from my first book *Imperfectly Natural Woman*.

I had big reservations. My instinct was that it was too niche to be a bestseller, and it would blow my big chance of becoming the new Gwyneth Paltrow, but I agreed. *Imperfectly Natural Baby and Toddler* was my second book, and despite many arguments with the editor who wanted to play safe with everything it did OK. Zero PR, though, and this time I paid a PR agency myself, which was another disaster. They sent me copies of their 'activities' weekly – a list of publications they had allegedly reached out to, who had said no, or not yet. It was so depressing. I personally knew one of the magazines they'd allegedly pitched the book to because I'd written for them when *Imperfectly Natural Woman* was flying high. The journalist wrote me a lovely email back. 'I didn't know about your new book, I've asked about, no one has been sent a copy, do feel free to send it along.' Honestly, no wonder PR has such a bad rap. Truth is, the wrangles with the original publisher had given the new publisher cold feet. The baby book was niche. It was never going to be as big as my original A–Z idea, and at the time I felt that the chance to capitalise on the momentum of *Imperfectly Natural Woman* had been lost. In hindsight, I should have stuck to my guns. After the baby book, the next book with the new publisher was, most probably, just a contractual obligation. I was excited for my new editor to come back to work with me, but just as it came time to discuss it, she disappeared off on maternity leave again. More babies than me!

I didn't let it stop me, though. With the big publishing advance and Radio 2, along with Simon having his busiest ever year composing TV music, things were good. I'd become a freelance journalist and was writing for a fair number of publications. I'd really found my flow. I loved writing about holistic living, and the world of woo-woo was opening.

Chapter 32
TIME TO GO

I was back on *The Big Show* when Lulu was about three months old. I found a childminder who lived in St Johns Wood, so I'd drive there, find somewhere to park (the stressful bit!) and leave Lulu with her for a few hours while I was at work. It was only three days a week, it worked OK, but on the other days, Simon had commitments and I had become a full-on taxi driver for getting Rocky to kindergarten, and Sonny and Buddy to various home educating activities or to NatureKids. It was all so bitty.

I'd done so much reading over the years about schools, and I was a big believer that five was too early for boys to start school, and that in the early years they needed to play. That was where the Steiner philosophy worked well: in Europe most children don't start the academic curriculum till they're six or seven and that is how Steiner schools in the UK operate too.

We knew of a Steiner school 10 miles away, but still in Hertfordshire. And after an open day, we could imagine the boys there. I loved their relaxed approach, and the kindergarten seemed wonderful for Lulu and Rocky. They all started that summer.

Simon and I took turns leaving ridiculously early in the morning to do the 45-minute drive in rush hour. One day, I was heading to pick the boys up after *The Big Show*, when there was some kind of accident on the motorway. The traffic reports – nowhere near as fun as the ones I'd done, though I say so myself – spoke of the whole area being gridlocked. I knew no one in the area and had no idea where the kids could go, if they weren't picked up on time. Stuck in that jam, I had lots of time to think. I started to imagine winter nights, snow and ice, maybe one of the boys needing to stay late. I imagined playdates and after-school stuff where one child needed to stay, and the other didn't. How could we navigate driving over to get one child, then having to drive back again, with another one in kindergarten coming up to school age himself, and a toddler? I could see myself spending half my life on the M25.

I prayed out loud. It must have worked, as the road opened and things started to flow, metaphorically and well as literally. I drove through the High Street and decided there and then that we'd move. We needed to be local, we needed to simplify our life and allow the kids the experience of walking to school. I could suddenly understand why parents moved to an area just to be near a school.

The estate agent actually laughed when I said I wanted to rent a large, 4- or 5-bed house with a garden near the school. 'I'll add you to the list,' he said. 'There are 10 families on it currently.' I had no idea the school and the area were so popular, and there were very few big properties other than some mansions on the road near the woods. Totally out of our price range, even with my nice book advance.

At a summer event at the school that weekend, we met some parents. There were so many like-minded people, it was wonderful; suddenly I'd found my tribe. I took along some homemade cacao energy balls and got chatting to some yummy mummies. It's a nightmare trying to find a house here, they agreed, but one said, 'My neighbour's house is up for grabs, the tenants are leaving soon, and I'm pretty sure the owners want to sell, not rent.'

We bought the house and planned to move in before school started in September. One memory that always makes me smile was looking around that house with Simon and Lulu while the boys were at school. The owner, a lovely older woman, sat by the pond in the garden, and told us: 'Feel free to look around.' I said to Lulu, 'Our family might be coming here, to live.' She looked puzzled, looked back at the owner and said, 'But what will we do with the lady?'

Leaving the Garden House was a huge wrench. We'd really made it our own, and we had amassed huge pieces of furniture that would clearly not fit our new home. Clearing it all out was a mammoth task.

I remember one Saturday while we were trying to navigate dealing with four kids while clearing out and packing (impossible when toddlers think taking something back out of a box is fantastic fun!). There was a knock on the door and a couple of our friends, Karen and Ben, both university professors, stood there in 'decorating clothes' and said: 'We've come to help, you have us both for the day, just show us what needs to be done.' OMG, they were saviours. That's kindness right there.

I will never forget the day we left our Hatfield home for the last time. We had emptied the house, cleaned it and even done a bit of a space clearing. I'm a big believer that it's important to thank a home and shift the energy before you leave for the next residents. Simon had left in his car to follow the furniture truck, the boys were in school and Lulu was with our au pair. I put my bag in the car and popped back into the hall to say one last goodbye to the house. As I stood there, I felt a very strange sensation, and then saw what I can only describe as spirits/entities: I couldn't identify a shape, but they were flying in front of me and they seemed to be saying: *Don't leave*. It was not so much frightening, as incredibly sad. I don't think the house wanted us to leave. I said out loud: 'Thank you for such wonderful years. We have to go now.'

I had to drop some stuff off at a friend on the way to our new home 'Oh dear,' she said, 'you look like you've seen a ghost!' 'I have,' I replied shakily, 'several of them I think.'

Years later, I found myself back at Hatfield House and couldn't resist sneaking a look at the Garden House. It was empty, left exactly as the day we'd left – in fact, I walked around to the garden and there in the corner, a crate of bottles that we had forgotten to clear away after our leaving party was growing moss. The house looked desolate. It made me cry.

Chapter 33
HARDCORE WOO-WOO

Having four children, you can imagine I had a lot of views to share on Steve's show: he would regularly quiz me on all things natural parenting, and we had some huge laughs, arguing about natural remedies.

Steve would often say, 'I like the idea of your Echinacea for a cold, but it takes four weeks to kick in!'

As the years passed, and with each baby, I became more and more conscious of holistic health. I don't much like the word *holistic*, but it really is the only one that explains it. From my twenties I had become aware that I didn't buy into the *pill for every ill* mentality, and watching my dad become a walking pharmacy (he'd have loved to get his hands on Steve's US stash), I knew that I'd take a different path.

I became a great fan of Louise Hay and pretty much all the Hay House books, so when I got an opportunity to become a Hay House author in 2014 it was a dream come true. I signed to Hay House and wrote *Look Great Naturally . . . without ditching the lipstick*. It included lots of DIY recipes for natural skincare, lots of cosmetics, and a whole section on mindset. There were chapters on yoga, meditation and therapeutic treatments, and while the book didn't hit the bestsellers list, it changed my career in some important ways. For starters I got to speak at Hay House conferences alongside some of the greats – Dr David Hamilton, Robert Holden, Sonia Choquette et al. – and I felt part of the Hay House family. For a couple of years, I presented a weekly show for Hay House Radio US – looking back, that was awesome. I got to interview most of their authors, including the great Julia Cameron, author of *The Artist's Way*.

Julia made an impression on me, for sure. She was once married to Martin Scorsese, and shared that she had no less than 48 rejections for her first novel (never give up!) and that *The Artist's Way* is a multi-million international bestseller.

Becoming part of the Hay House author family immersed me even more into the world of woo. The truth was, I knew pretty much everything I needed to when it came to meditation, mindset, spirituality: I'd interviewed all the experts, and read all the books. But a fair bit of it didn't feel real to me. I also had the tricky job of squaring it with my Christian faith.

For years, I spoke about and taught the spiritual stuff, did yoga retreats, attended gong baths, shamanic healing rituals, cacao ceremonies, etc., but there was always a bit of me that felt that I wasn't being quite authentic, that I was observing myself trying to be woo-woo but it didn't feel real.

There is no doubt I was on a path of healing. I was constantly searching for something. When Lulu was around three, I decided to go on a retreat with Jason Vale, the Juice Master, in Turkey and it was a game changer. It really underlined for me the importance of looking at the whole picture when it comes to health – the holistic picture, rather than the *Quick Fix approach*.

I'd seen it played out so clearly over the years with my dad. I'd seen him subconsciously create illnesses, possibly so that he could get a break from the stress of my mum's mental illness. He dutifully took every drug prescribed, and then more to counteract the effects of those. Nothing ever got any better, though. His symptoms were treated, but he didn't ever seek the root cause. I suspect his mental health issues were not, in fact, treatable with statins or 'water pills'. In more recent years I've felt very sad about what I didn't know back then; perhaps I could have persuaded him to try a different approach.

I became great friends with Jason, and he came into the *Steve Wright in the Afternoon* show a couple of times. For some reason he really wound Wrighty up. I can only assume his jovial optimism, and determination that juice was the answer, was irritating. Jason invited Steve on juice retreats along with Gary Barlow, Carol Vorderman and Amanda Holden, but of course Steve didn't take him up on the offer. Jason would bring in a flask of cold, freshly pressed juice when he came in to be interviewed, but I ended up drinking it all usually. Sadly, Steve was of the *keep taking the pills* mentality, rather than being open to the idea of looking at the holistic picture.

In Turkey for a Juicy Retreat

Chapter 34
RIP GEORGE MICHAEL

It was Christmas Day 2016 when I got a call to say that George Michael had died. While I was reeling from the shock, calls were coming in from radio and TV to share some memories. I did a few radio interviews then, but over the course of the next couple of years, I was invited to do more in-depth pieces for documentaries about his life. One TV company sent a camera crew to my home. I knew they were digging for dirt, so I cut to the quick and told the producer I was happy to appear, but I could only share my experiences of the Wham! tours, which were all fantastic – and if they were after some sensationalism around George, I was not going to dish any dirt because there was none. *That's fine*, they said, *we want it to be a lovely tribute to George*. They came along, filmed me and left saying, 'That was great'. When I later watched the documentary on TV, much of my footage had ended up on the cutting room floor – and lo and behold, they'd managed to find a few talking heads to say something derogatory. I was asked to be in a show for ABC television too. I didn't ever get to see it, and again, I might have been cut out. It's tricky if you accept a gig and later find out that their agenda is not all they promised.

Along with the rest of the world I loved the Netflix 2023 doc *WHAM!*. I thought it beautifully portrayed the close friendship of George and Andy, and of course my family laughed out loud at the shots of the gigs, where you can see me bobbing about with my huge '80s hairstyle.

I could barely catch my breath with grief again when I heard of George's sister Melanie's death, exactly three years later, on Christmas Day. She was only 59. Heartbreaking.

Chapter 35
COOL BY ASSOCIATION

I was never famous. I'm quite grateful that, unlike Steve, I didn't get clocked in the street. There were, however, a few funny occasions when people recognised my voice. I rang a local tourist board in Devon once and asked if they had any properties available for a week's rental for a family. The reply? 'Is that Janey Lee Grace? I recognise your voice.'

My kids of course couldn't care less that their mum worked in the radio, until the opportunity came along that they might meet someone famous. I got the chance to be a cool mum when certain footballers, actors or, later, YouTubers came into the show and I was able to get an autograph or a signed book.

Anyone remember the very first YouTube influencer who made it big? Charlieissocoollike. Yep, Charlie MacDonnell, vlogger and filmmaker, whose YouTube channel, I believe, was the first to hit one million subscribers in 2011. He (now'she') had started the trend. Not long after it was Alfie Deye, who also became an influencing megastar. Rocky and Buddy were both desperate to meet him. In fact, they'd recently queued for no less than five hours outside Waterstones in Piccadilly for a book signing, only to be told by security, no more people were being allowed in. Apparently 8000 kids had turned up! So, my kids were lucky enough to come in and meet him, and also Marcus Butler, who was lovely – as was Steve who welcomed this new brand of social media stars into the studio. Rocky, ever the confident force to be reckoned with, came in and sat next to me and Tim. Steve said: 'You're welcome to ask Marcus a question if you like.' He did. What a claim to fame if he ever wanted to follow in my footsteps: being on national radio aged nine!

Steve occasionally mentioned the kids on the show in one way or another. One day when we opened the mics to do a talky bit, I could see the phone ringing, and said to Steve who saw me looking at the phone, 'Sorry, it's my son, he's just had his driving test.' 'Put him on!' Steve said, so I took the call live on air, to an excited Buddy who had passed, thank goodness! It wouldn't have made such good radio if we'd all been commiserating. The same happened with Lulu's GCSE results – announced live on air!

On one Christmas I rocked up to work to find some excitement in the production team because Will Ferrell was coming in: we were going to be seeing Buddy the Elf in person! He ended up staying for the whole show and joining us for talky bits and factoids. The kids were incensed that I hadn't taken them in to meet him. That same year, Millie Bobby Brown was coming in to be interviewed. I asked the producers if Sonny and Rocky, both *Stranger Things* fans, could come in and meet her. *Of course*, they said, *no problem*. For once, I'd be a cool mum. That buzz was spectacularly killed when I got a text from the producer the night before the show to say that she had pulled. Apparently, her parents felt she needed to take some time out, so she was dropping some promotional interviews from the schedule.

I let the boys read the message, otherwise it would all be my fault again. For a little while they both quipped: 'Millie Bobbie Brown's parents ruined my life.'

Simon was furious with me one day too, as I arrived at work to find Carole King playing Elton's piano in the green room, doing an actual live session. He is one of her biggest fans and would have loved to meet her. She signed an album for him, though; that had to do.

There were also two Christmas periods when I was far from cool, according to my kids. I was offered a role in pantomime to play the Spirit of the Ring in *Aladdin*, in

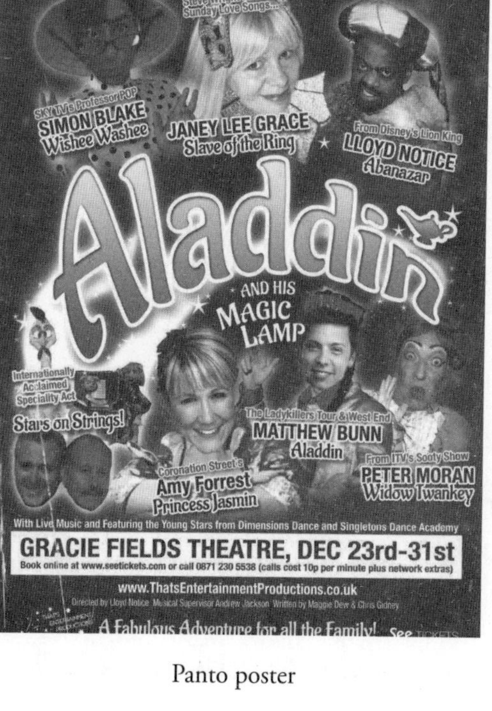

Panto poster

Rochdale of all places. The kids were still young, and I had a lot of commitments, so my initial response was to say no.

The producer asked me to think about it for a couple of days. During that time I had so much stress, with my mum's mental health and a whole load of difficulties with my kids' school, I decided I needed some TLC and booked a back massage. The masseur decided that I was clearly wound up. She told me that her happiest clients (she worked a lot with actors and musicians) were those who did pantomime every year. That did it for me. I signed up, and despite the hideous journey and the far from ideal accommodation in Rochdale, I LOVED it. I hadn't done any stage acting since college days, so I was a little outside of my comfort

In panto as the Spirit of the Ring in *Aladdin*

zone, but I loved the camaraderie among the cast and the fabulous choreography. The script was adapted to include a few factoids for me, of course, and there was the odd nod to being on Steve Wright's show.

The costumes were pretty fab too, except that I was given no guidance over what shoes to wear. I opted for shiny, red, high-heeled shoes with a strap, which seemed fine till the night that my whole family drove up to see me perform. The cast knew that my husband, mum and four kids (two young teenagers) were in the audience, so they vowed to crack a few personal jokes, make sure I made an impression, and generally have a laugh. They didn't need to: in the heavily choreographed ensemble number in Act I, I sang my heart out and sashayed across the stage, only to catch my heel in my billowing Turkish pants. I went skidding across the stage, literally arse over tit, and the whole cast had to try not to laugh as I picked myself up and tried to carry on as if nothing had happened. There really is nothing funnier than someone falling over, so long as it's not you!

The following year I did it all again (in lower heeled shoes!) and starred as the Fairy Godmother in *Cinderella*, much closer to home in Cambridgeshire. I was due to play that role again in 2020 on the Isle of Wight, but of course we all know what went down that Christmas, and sadly the theatre couldn't open.

If you're from the US or Canada reading this, you may find it hard to understand why pantomime is so entertaining (*Oh no you don't!*). It really is quintessentially British and for someone like me who loves singing, dancing and generally showing off, it's perfect.

Chapter 36
THE BUZZ WITHOUT THE BOOZE

At Radio 2 parties I'd regularly get a bit tipsy, and Steve and Tim would quip, 'We love Janey when she has taken a drink.' I don't know if I was worse than anyone else – I doubt it, we could all put some booze away – but it was certainly affecting me even though I was in denial.

The ironic bit is that as well as being the queen of holistic living, the one banging on about organic food, supplements, therapeutic techniques, self-care, etc., I was also downing the best part of a bottle of wine most nights.

I'd wake, usually around 3 a.m. (the time for liver repair!) with my heart beating and the ceiling spinning, and I'd hear a voice saying: *This isn't right. You're supposed to care about the holistic picture, what are you doing? This isn't authentic with who you're meant to be.* I'd make a deal with God in those small hours, and pray: 'Please let me be OK, no hangover, I've got a really busy day....and in return I promise I'll stop drinking.'

God kept his side of the bargain. I rarely had hangovers, never had a day off work sick in 24 years – but sadly and despite declaring that I'd quit, by 6 p.m. the sun was over the yardarm, and I'd head to the local wine bar and have a 'treat', a nice cold Sauvignon, then back home for more with dinner.

I was never at rock bottom – the expression is *high bottomed* (I wish) – but I was caught in the alcohol trap. In our culture we're brainwashed into thinking that there are only two types of drinkers: those at rock bottom, who need clinical support or rehab, and everyone else, happy social drinkers who sometimes just can't hold their beer. The reality is, it's a spectrum. It's not black or white: the phrase used by Jolene Park in her TEDx talk is 'Gray Area Drinking'. I didn't know how to get free from the alcohol trap. Surely, I wouldn't be able to have fun, chill out, relax, be happy without my wine? But being on Steve's show proved to be monumental in my sobriety journey.

This was kick-started at the end of 2017, when we were given a book by Clare Pooley to read over the Christmas break. We rarely had one night to look at a book, so two weeks was unusual. I looked at the title, *The Sober Diaries*, and I just knew this book would change me. Of course, I didn't read it straight away, I didn't want to spoil Christmas, but I started the book on the 28th, stopped drinking on the 30th (I offered to drive to a New Year's Eve party) and then figured I'd do Dry January and tell Clare when she came in.

I never looked back; my only regret is not doing it sooner.

Clare became a friend, and I invited her back to talk about her new novel. Then I invited Catherine Gray onto the show to talk about *The Unexpected Joy of Being Sober* and her subsequent two books. Lots of people have told me they heard me speaking about ditching the booze on air, or they heard one of the guests who inspired them to follow suit. In 2019 I gave a TEDx talk 'Sobriety Rocks – Who Knew!'

The Sober Club is launched

and after that day, when I realised that there were so many people in the same position, I started The Sober Club, a community for the sober curious and those already sober to focus on wellbeing.

So, with sobriety as my theme, it was time for another book: *Happy Healthy Sober: Ditch the booze and take control of your life.*

Chapter 37
THE WOO, AND THE OTHER WOO

As you've seen, there has been a fair smattering of the woo-woo across my life. There isn't much I haven't got involved in – from shamanic healing, through yoga, breathwork, gong baths, cacao ceremonies and all manner of therapies to energy healing, reiki, theta healing, hypnosis, etc. – but I pride myself of on always having one foot firmly on the ground.

Being spiritual to me means acknowledging that there's more to life than just what meets the eye. It's about recognising and honouring a sense of connection to something greater than myself, whether that's nature, the universe or a higher power. (For me, that is Christianity, but I realise that others recognise another 'source'.)

I don't call it religion, though. I think spirituality is the deep dive to knowing yourself on a deeper level. I don't know how I'd have coped in my fearful years without that belief. I was always insecure, knowing I had no safety net of supportive parents, and unsure how I'd ever make anything of myself with just my own resources.

Self-love is the foundational piece, really. I've had to learn to find a way to accept myself fully, flaws and all, and treat myself with kindness and compassion. So, while some may dismiss these ideas as woo-woo, I see them as practical tools grounded in both ancient wisdom and modern research for living a happier, more fulfilling life.

But the word *woo* means something else too…

I'd always been interested in 'personality tools', and when I finished touring with Wham!, I wondered what the future held for me career-wise. I did the Myers-Briggs Type Indicator test, just for fun. This personality type test showed that I was an 'off the scale' extrovert. I didn't even want to have a bath without the door open so that I could chat to flatmates. More recently I've come across another assessment tool called CliftonStrengths, developed by Gallup. (You've heard of Gallup polls?) The assessment helps figure out what someone is good at by asking them pertinent questions. My assessment showed that I have 'WOO' as a high-ranking strength. *How come they include that?* I thought. *How can they know from those questions that I love my crystals and meditation?*

Of course, in the CliftonStrengths assessment, WOO doesn't refer to the 'out there' in any way. It stands for 'Winning Others Over' and means that I excel in connecting with people, building relationships and influencing others positively.

Well, that sounds like me – right? I am both out there woo-woo, and high ranking at WOO – Winning Others Over. I'll take that.

Chapter 38
THE END OF AN ERA

The Big Show ended officially on 31 September 2022, but really the heart went out of it for me in March 2020, the last time we were all in the studio together on a regular basis. Once lockdown happened, we had to find a way to continue doing the show but online. Tim and I linked up from our respective homes and Steve 'drove the desk' on his own in the studio at Radio 2. All the guests came down the line, and it was hard to get the same interaction. I think we did OK, but we longed to get back into the studio. We went back for a few shows, but on 22 March we were officially given the news. It was a shocker, but good of the BBC to give us plenty of warning. Wrighty fully intended to get another afternoon show. 'I want us to move stations as a team,' he said, so a waiting game began. He didn't want to reveal the news till the summer, so when he finally did, I'd known about it for months. I don't think he was expecting quite the furore to be honest. Listeners were furious. When on TV sharing his reaction to the news, Steve was dignified, and said, 'I've had a good run, sometimes people want you, sometimes they don't.'

But he was devastated, without doubt. The rumours that he had simply retired were wholly untrue. Wrighty lived and breathed radio – BBC Radio 2 to be precise.

On the day of the very last show, it was unbelievably emotional. We weren't in at the station, so it was literally business as usual, and he signed off with a big thank you to the audience. On the Radio 2 website page he said:

> *I know I've been extremely lucky to do this work and have never taken it for granted.… There is no truth in the rumour I'm planning to open my own artisan bakery, and I've turned down twice the chance to open my own nail bar. So, it's all good. Please do listen to Scott Mills and Sara Cox when they take over afternoons. They are both brilliant broadcasters and I truly wish them well when they start.*

Ever the pro.

Life without Radio 2 took some getting used to. I hadn't been doing many hours from home, so it wasn't a massive change in my daily routine, though I was glad to be free from the hours of research and factoid collection, but the biggest change came in the lack of fun in my life. Until it ended, I don't think I had realised just how much we laughed on that show. Steve was very, very, funny, and after a few weeks of our show ending, I realised that I was simply not using my facial muscles as much, not laughing!

* * *

For the last 20 or so years, I had become much more involved in my mum's life. Due to her mental illness, we had a tricky relationship. In truth she pressed every button with me because I never really had the mothering I needed. None of that was her fault, of course; her own mother had died when she was young and even though I'd had lots of therapeutic sessions, nothing seemed to be able to sort out my angst around my own lack of parenting.

When my children were young, I came across Family Constellations, and went along to a workshop with an open mind. I told the practitioner that I didn't feel I was a good enough mother, so she set about looking at the energetic picture of my family system. It was incredibly powerful. In one short 40-minute session my whole view of my mother changed: I could see clearly that she had literally done her best, but that she had nothing much to give. She had,

With Steve at Hyde Park

however, given me life, and given me enough to be me. I was able to honour that, and it was life-changing. After that, even my own children noticed that 'Mum doesn't argue with Grandma anymore'.

Aside from her bipolar, my mum had been strong and physically well. She had some mobility issues in her late eighties which meant she had to go into a care home, but she made it to the ripe old age of 94. A fall, and the subsequent hospitalisation, led to her demise. I am so grateful I got to spend time with her and can't help but smile at the very last words she ever said to me, in her half-conscious state: 'Will you be OK now the radio has ended?'

She died in December 2022. My sister and I were trying to sort out her funeral but got held back by various bits of red tape. It was becoming ridiculous, but we finally buried her late February 2023, in the beautiful woodland plot that she had arranged, booked and paid for many years earlier without any of us knowing. She had always loved daffodils, and I am quite sure she intervened so that the burial would be a sunny day with the daffs in bloom. RIP Norma.

* * *

Even without *The Big Show*, life continued to be hectic. The Sober Club was getting bigger every day, and I was training Sober Coaches, running courses, speaking at events, running my Platinum Awards for natural products and, of course, writing – including this memoir and a (yet to be published) novel. Although I did a regular spot on UK Health Radio, a bit of me still pined for mainstream radio. Steve would sometimes call me out of the blue. He had been in touch with this or that station, lots of them wanted *The Big Show*. He had got some offers, and I was to 'hang on in there', but he said it was a good job he wasn't full-time at that point he was looking after his dad a fair bit. I wasn't holding out any hopes.

On World Radio Day, I wrote a blog post for my social media which looked back at the post I'd written when *The Big Show* ended. It included the story of how I met Steve, how much fun we had on the show, the favourite guests, the junkets, and the days out. I reminisced about *Ready Steady Cook* and *Celebrity Antiques Road Trip* with Tim. I wrote a bit about *Steve Wright's Sunday Love Songs* and thanked both the listeners and the producers. I gave an update as to what I was doing a year on. I uploaded that post to LinkedIn and Facebook mid-afternoon and as I did so, my phone pinged, and I learned of Steve's death. What an awful, awful shock. I was sobbing and shaking as the phone calls came in from radio and TV stations wanting me to comment. It was all too hard, but in the coming days I was interviewed on *BBC Breakfast*, Sky and lots of radio stations, paying tribute to by boss and friend of so many years. The outpouring of grief was incredible. I think Steve really would have been blown away. We knew he was beloved, but I don't think he knew to what extent. I wrote another blog post the next day called Steve Wright and me… Reflections, which I have included towards the end of this book for you to read.

Chapter 39
LIFE GOES ON

Quitting the booze at the start of 2018 had opened up so much more energy and clarity for me. I was already working as a media and PR coach, but quickly realised there was more skills that could be beneficial for me, so I trained as an Emotional Freedom Technique (EFT) practitioner. (Lots of people are now aware of EFT, after Boy George was seen tapping to reduce anxiety in the jungle on *I'm a Celebrity...Get Me Out Of Here!*) That led to training in Matrix Reimprinting, which is a fantastic modality that uses EFT but which goes one step further to allow us to literally reframe our 'baggage' and reduce the impact of limiting beliefs and trauma. I then trained as an NLP practitioner (neurolinguistic programming) and as a health and recovery coach. In more recent years I've trained in the aforementioned Family Constellations, which is tricky to describe (watch the Netflix series *Another Life*) but incredibly powerful.

What's up now? At the time of writing, I've never been busier, and sometimes wonder how I ever found time to go to the BBC to work. I'm doing radio shows online, my own health and wellbeing shows, and my very popular (though I do say so) podcast *Alcohol Free Life*. The Sober Club online is rocking, and I'm coaching clients one-to-one, running Family Constellations workshops and heart-centred business days, plus training people to be holistic sober coaches. I'm also still a freelance writer and speaker.

I love it all, but the truth is, as well as not laughing as much, and apart from treading the boards in the pantos and auto-lurching into some backing vocals when Wham! comes on the radio, I don't sing enough! The latter is an easy fix; Simon can always think of something where some female vocals are needed! And any record or panto producers reading this, I'm your girl! For the laughter, without Wrighty's wit, I guess I'm just going to have to make my own fun.

I do believe you can choose happiness. Naturally, I can be a terribly anxious worrier, and prone to negativity, but I do spend my life, ya know, WOO (Winning Others Over) and usually inspiring people to focus on gratitude, purpose, self-esteem and happiness, so I guess the key is to point a few fingers back at myself.

It's hard to summarise my life lessons (if you can see a theme here, let me know!), but I think the one thing I want to be is happy in my own skin. Despite my age, I can't imagine retiring. I still have the excitement of Tigger about a new project – and still can't resist a great pop tune. With all my years on the mic in music and radio, I always have an earworm, usually something terrible that drives me crazy, but right now, as I have been reminiscing, it's one of Wham!'s finest:

> *'Sometimes you wake up in the morning with a bass line, a ray of sunshine...and you're ready to go!'*

I'll take that.

STEVE WRIGHT AND ME... REFLECTIONS

BY JANEY LEE GRACE – FEBRUARY 18, 2024

I've dedicated the Alcohol Free Life podcast on the week of Steve's passing to a tribute to my friend and 'boss' for 24 years.

The irony was not lost on me... Tuesday 13 Feb was World Radio Day and I was responding to some comments on my social media post about just how much I miss being on Steve Wright in the Afternoon. *Our show ended late 2022 and for someone addicted to radio (it is indeed addictive) it's been a tough adjustment. A message pinged into my inbox followed by several more,....and I flicked over to a news page only to recoil in horror.*

'Steve Wright, legendary broadcaster has died suddenly aged 69'.

What a shock, and a devastating loss. I had a massive weep, and rang my former co-host Tim Smith and then I had to get my act together to appear on Sky News to pay tribute. The next day or so saw me on various radio stations and Good Morning Britain *alongside Tony Blackburn to share thoughts about Steve, and what he meant to us.*

One of the comments on my social media said: 'He was the sound of my life,' I couldn't have put it better, I loved Steve Wright growing up, as a wannabe pop star I attended Radio 1 road shows, and when 'Cola Boy' hit Number 8 in the pop charts, I was really disappointed not to meet him on Top of the Pops.

Steve really was a legend in broadcasting. Renowned for his long-standing career in radio, he has left an indelible mark on the industry and the hearts of his listeners. His charisma is often cited as one of his most memorable traits. We all loved him for his timeless wit and humour. He was very relatable, with lots of clever one-liners and playful interactions with callers, and he kept audiences entertained for decades.

He was innovative and initiated the 'zoo' format in radio [in the UK]. Lots of recent tributes from celebrities said that he was the reason they worked in TV and Radio. He was doing it for 40 years, and he lived and breathed radio. I've never met anyone in radio so hard-working, and he was something of a perfectionist. He was always so relatable, he wanted to be across the zeitgeist and he kept everyone entertained – from the truck driver, the parents on the school run, the factory workers…. my old mum in her care home. Steve was funny, both on and off air.

Being a co-host on Steve Wright in the Afternoon *changed my life in so many ways. I had young children and was sharing stuff about my growing passion for holistic living, organic food, skincare without chemicals etc. – all of which morphed into a 'second career'.*

When the show came to an end in 2022 I can't pretend we weren't all more than a little heartbroken. It really was the end of an era, and there was a huge outpouring of love for the show, and lots of people encouraging the BBC to rethink their decision!

In this podcast I share some thoughts on grief, and how none of us know how long we have got left! They used to say we'd have '3 score and 10' (70 years). Of course most of us hope for 20 or 30 more. Poor Steve only made it to 69, but once we recognise how precious our time is, we have to stop procrastinating and do what we love.

RIP Steve. I miss you.

FACTOIDS

...for the '80s, '90s and early 2000s

The 1980s saw the rise of MTV, making music videos popular.

Live Aid, the concert organised by Bob Geldof and Midge Ure and held in 1985, raised millions for famine relief in Ethiopia and featured performances by some of the biggest acts of the 1980s.

The term *yuppie* (young urban professional) became popular in the 1980s to describe affluent, career-driven young people.

The Walkman was originally called Sound-about in the US, and Stowaway in the UK, then Sony named it officially after the Pressman audio recorder featured in the *Superman* films.

Michael Jackson's album *Thriller*, released in 1982, became the bestselling album of all time, giving him his status as the King of Pop.

Fashion trends of the 1980s included power suits with padded shoulders, leg warmers, neon colours, and oversized accessories, but there was also a penchant for avant-garde glossy rubber clothing and futuristic studded accessories, including belts, bracelets and jackets.

British pop culture embraced futuristic themes and aesthetics inspired by sci-fi films like *Blade Runner* and *Star Wars*.

Waterbeds became a popular luxury item: 20 per cent of all mattress sales in 1987 were waterbeds.

British television series such as *EastEnders* and *Only Fools and Horses* became cultural phenomena during the 1980s.

Beanie Babies captured the imagination of children and collectors worldwide, leading to widespread merchandise and media franchises.

The New Romantic movement emerged from the nightclubs of London and Birmingham in the late 1970s, and along with British fashion designer Vivienne Westwood played a significant role in shaping the New Wave fashion of the 1980s.

The emergence of electronic dance music genres such as acid house and techno paved the way for the rave culture of the late '80s and early '90s.

The popularity of home video game consoles like the ZX Spectrum and Commodore 64 soared during the 1980s, leading to a golden age of gaming.

The emergence of supermodels like Naomi Campbell and Cindy Crawford in the 1980s reshaped the fashion industry.

Spandau Ballet, Duran Duran, Culture Club, the Human League, Wham!, Pet Shop Boys, Tears for Fears, the

Eurythmics, Bananarama, Simple Minds and U2 — all had huge fame through the 1980s.

1990s

The 1990s saw the rise of the internet and the mainstream adoption of personal computers, leading to significant changes in communication, entertainment and commerce.

Grunge music emerged as a dominant genre in the early 1990s, with bands like Nirvana, Pearl Jam and Soundgarden defining the sound and style of the decade.

Pokémon and Tamagotchi captured the imagination of children and collectors worldwide, leading to widespread merchandise and media franchises.

The popularity of boy bands and girl groups soared in the 1990s, with acts like Backstreet Boys, *NSYNC and Destiny's Child dominating the charts.

Hip-hop culture continued to thrive and diversify in the 1990s, with artists like Tupac Shakur, The Notorious B.I.G., Dr. Dre and Wu-Tang Clan.

The 1990s witnessed the explosion of alternative rock, with bands like Radiohead, Smashing Pumpkins and Red Hot Chili Peppers.

The emergence of reality television shows like *The Real World*, *Big Brother* and *Survivor* revolutionised the TV landscape and influenced future programming trends.

The 1990s witnessed significant advancements in technology, including the widespread adoption of mobile phones, CD-ROMs and the development of early versions of social media platforms.

The Spice Girls took the world by storm in the mid-1990s with their colourful personas and catchy pop tunes, including hits like 'Wannabe' and 'Spice Up Your Life'.

Oasis became one of the biggest bands of the 1990s Britpop movement with albums like *Definitely Maybe* and *(What's the Story) Morning Glory?* featuring anthems like 'Wonderwall' and 'Don't Look Back in Anger.'

Early 2000s

The early 2000s marked the proliferation of reality television shows, with series like *American Idol*, *The Osbournes* and *The Bachelor*. The rise of social media platforms like MySpace and Friendster in the early 2000s laid the groundwork for the digital age, transforming the way people connect and share content online.

Pop-punk and emo music surged in popularity during the early 2000s, with bands like Blink-182, Green Day, My Chemical Romance and Fall Out Boy.

The influence of hip-hop continued to grow in the early 2000s, with artists like Eminem, Jay-Z, Nelly, and OutKast achieving mainstream success.

The emergence of reality talent shows like *American Idol* provided a platform for aspiring singers to launch their careers, leading to the discovery of stars like Kelly Clarkson, Carrie Underwood and Jennifer Hudson.

Fashion trends of the early 2000s included low-rise jeans, velour tracksuits, chunky highlights and trucker hats, reflecting a mix of nostalgia and contemporary styles.

The *Harry Potter* book series by J.K. Rowling became a global phenomenon in the early 2000s, inspiring the successful film franchise.

The September 11 terrorist attacks in 2001 had a profound impact on global culture and politics, leading to increased security measures, changes in media coverage and shifts in public perception.

The popularity of mobile phones and portable music devices like the iPod revolutionised how people consume media and stay connected on the go.

Superhero films experienced a resurgence in the early 2000s, with franchises like *Spider-Man*, *X-Men* and *The Dark Knight* paving the way for future blockbuster successes.

Britney Spears was one of the biggest pop stars of the early 2000s, and Beyoncé also rose to prominence as a solo artist following the breakup of Destiny's Child.

MY FAVOURITE '80s – SINGLES PLAYLIST

Wake Me Up Before You Go-Go – Wham! 1984

Girls Just Want to Have Fun – Cyndi Lauper 1983

Little Red Corvette – Prince 1983

Wouldn't It Be Good – Nik Kershaw 1984

You Are My World – The Communards 1987

If You Let Me Stay – Terence Trent D'Arby 1987

Time After Time – Cyndi Lauper 1983

Fast Car – Tracy Chapman 1988

Walking on Sunshine – Katrina and the Waves 1985

Come On Eileen – Dexys Midnight Runners 1982

Just What I Always Wanted – Mari Wilson 1982

Mary's Prayer – Danny Wilson 1987

Take On Me – a-ha 1985

Every Breath You Take – The Police 1983

Everybody Wants to Rule the World –
Tears for Fears 1985

Luka – Suzanne Vega 1987

Running Up That Hill – Kate Bush 1985

Talk of the Town – Pretenders: 1980

With or Without You – U2 1987

Let's Dance – David Bowie 1983

Money for Nothing – Dire Straits 1985

Call Me – Blondie 1980

Every Time You Go Away – Paul Young 1985

A Ray of Sunshine – Wham! 1983

MY FAVOURITE '90's – SINGLES PLAYLIST

Freedom! '90 – George Michael 1990

Groove Is in the Heart – Deee-Lite 1990

This Year's Love – David Gray 1999

You Get What You Give – New Radicals 1998

Smells Like Teen Spirit – Nirvana 1991

Walking in Memphis – Marc Cohn 1991

Common People – Pulp 1995

Glory Box – Portishead 1994

Wonderwall – Oasis 1995

Brimful of Asha – Cornershop 1997

Torn – Natalie Imbruglia 1997

Movin' on Up – Primal Scream 1991

Two Princes – Spin Doctors 1993

Stars – Simply Red 1991

Shiny Happy People – R.E.M. 1991

Fields of Gold – Sting 1993

Welcome to Paradise – Green Day 1991

How Bizarre – OMC 1995

Hold On –Wilson Phillips 1990

Stay (I Missed You) – Lisa Loeb 1994

What's Up? – 4 Non Blondes 1993

Dreams – The Cranberries 1992

Virtual Insanity – Jamiroquai 1996

7 Ways to Love – Cola Boy 1991

12 RULES FOR WOO – WELL-BEING ACCORDING TO JANEY

In no particular order, and apropos to absolutely nothing, these opinions are my own, and you should seek professional advice before undertaking them!

1. Go after your dreams. If you want something badly enough, make it happen. Make it non-negotiable. Be persistent.
2. Never have a root canal – and if you have one, consider its safe removal with a biological dentist.
3. Talk back to the inner critic. You are 'enough'. Don't allow yourself to be taken over by imposter syndrome.
4. Do your own research when it comes to the right diet for you. Consider looking at the work of Dr Weston A. Price for a very thorough approach to a traditional diet.
5. Find your purpose and make time for it. Remember, it may be that your purpose is just to be happy. Imagine how much better the world would be if more people focused on that!
6. Be Kind. For the know-it-alls, remember what F. Scott Fitzgerald said: 'It's better to be kind, than right.'

7. Tell those who mean something to you, how grateful you are.
8. Practise gratitude. When you're feeling fed up, and down, think of the many things you're grateful for. Focus on the joy of little things.
9. Never eat anything low fat or low sugar, and avoid artificial sweeteners like the plague.
10. Don't compare yourself to others, as President Roosevelt said, 'Comparison is the thief of joy.'
11. Don't wait till tomorrow or when you retire to do the things you want to do. Start now. Jack Cranfield said: 'You don't have to get it perfect, you just have to get it going.'
12. Ditch the booze. Oh, how I wish I'd done that sooner!

ABOUT THE AUTHOR

Janey Lee Grace is known as a singer touring with many famous bands such as Wham! and Boy George and a top 10 hit in the 90's with Cola Boy. She later co-hosted on BBC Radio 2's *Steve Wright in the Afternoon* and also appeared on *Good Morning Britain*, *Celebrity Antiques Road Trip*, *The Wright Stuff*, *BBC Breakfast* and Sky TV Entertainment news. She is a best-selling author of a number of books including *Imperfectly Natural Women* ISBN 9781904424895 and *Happy Healthy Sober* ISBN 9780857162120 and now shares her experience and expertise on the benefits of sobriety.

ACKNOWLEDGEMENTS

It's tricky writing acknowledgements for a memoir, because many of the important and influential people in my life are already honoured within the text. So just a huge thanks to those who helped get this book together. It wouldn't have happened without Caroline and Andy at McNidder & Grace who persuaded me to write this book. I have been told many times to write these stories down, they're wasted at dinner parties for sure, but they actually got me off my backside to do it.

I took off at various times during the writing of this book, to get a clear head, and jog my own memory, so a big thank you to Bev, Alison, Lou and Greg at Hedley House Hotel in York, and to Carolyn and Christian who put up with me typing away, providing coffee and ginger biscuits, and making encouraging noises. Thanks to all my friends (way too many to mention) and Sober Club members who knew I was writing this book and spurred me on when I couldn't decide if a story was worth including. Someone wise once said, 'Don't tell us about your old boyfriends' but my friends agreed I did need to include some of that!

There are too many industry colleagues to mention, (though many do get a credit in the book) but to everyone who has worked with me over the years in the music biz and the radio world, I love you all, and I'm so grateful for the laughs along the way. Sadly a few of the most influential people in my life died way too early: radio producer Chris Whatmough, George Michael, and of course the legendary Steve Wright who I spent 24 glorious years working with at BBC Radio 2. I hold them all in my heart, and I've shed a few tears writing about the way they impacted my life.

Of course I must say thank you to my wonderful family, I am SO blessed to have gorgeous grown up kids Sonny, Buddy, Rocky and Lulu. I hope you enjoy reading of my escapades from when I was your age. It's hard to imagine your old mum having that much fun! And of course, I couldn't have done any of this without my amazing husband Simon, my soul mate, my best friend, my business partner, and literally the wind beneath …and all that!

Janey Lee Grace
Summer 2024